20TH CENTURY Pop Culture

THE 90^s

Produced by Carlton Books

20 Mortimer Street

London, W1N 7RD

First published in hardback edition in 2001 by Chelsea House Publishers, a subsidiary of

Haights Cross Communications. Printed and bound in Dubai.

3 5 7 8 6 4 2

The Chelsea House World Wide Web address is http://www.chelseahouse.com

Library of Congress Cataloging-in-Publication Data applied for

The Early Years –1949   ISBN: 0-7910-6084-5

The 50s   ISBN: 0-7910-6085-3

The 60s   ISBN: 0-7910-6086-1

The 70s   ISBN: 0-7910-6087-X

The 80s   ISBN: 0-7910-6088-8

The 90s   ISBN: 0-7910-6089-6

20TH CENTURY

Pop Culture

THE 90s

Dan Epstein

Chelsea House Publishers

Philadelphia

20TH CENTURY

Pop Culture

The Early Years to 1949

The 50s

The 60s

The 70s

The 80s

Contents

1990 6

1991 10

1992 14

1993 18

1994 22

1995 26

1996 30

1997 34

1998 40

1999 44

Index 47

Acknowledgements/About the Author 48

'90

The recession of 1990, after the boom of the 1980s, provided a rather inauspicious beginning to the new decade. By the end of the year, unemployment was up, sales of new homes were down by a whopping 17.5 percent, the Gross National Product improved only 0.9 percent from 1989, and economists were forecasting more of the same for 1991. The US population hit 249 million in 1990, an increase of 23 million over the last decade. For the first time ever, over fifty percent of Americans were living in metropolitan areas.

TOP TELEVISION SHOWS

Cheers
Roseanne
The Cosby Show
A Different World
60 Minutes

ACADEMY AWARDS

BEST PICTURE
Dances with Wolves
directed by Kevin Costner

BEST ACTOR
Jeremy Irons
Reversal of Fortune

BEST ACTRESS
Kathy Bates
Misery

Not that big cities were necessarily any safer to live in; during the year, murder rates hit record highs in Dallas, Memphis, Milwaukee, New York, Phoenix, San Antonio, and Washington DC.

Saturnalia

With sales of new cars down 5.1 percent, the time seemed totally wrong for General Motors to introduce Saturn, its first new brand name in over sixty years. Saturn wasn't just another American car, however; designed specifically to lure younger buyers back from Honda, Toyota and other Japanese brands, Saturn combined the quality construction of its foreign counterparts with a customer-friendly approach. A "no ups, no extras" sales policy meant that customers were guaranteed a fair shake from Saturn dealers; if dissatisfied with the car for any reason, a buyer could return it before thirty days or fifteen hundred miles, no questions asked. Saturn quickly became the industry leader in car sales per dealer, causing other American companies to reconsider (at least briefly) their lackadaisical attitude towards customer satisfaction.

Dirty Photos?

In Cincinnati, the city's Contemporary Art Center faced an indictment for obscenity, in connection with an exhibit of photographs by that perennial right-wing favorite, Robert Mapplethorpe. The case marked the first time that a museum or its director faced such charges; both were acquitted by a jury in October.

Rock World Rocked

A record store clerk in Florida was arrested for selling a 2 Live Crew abum to a minor; in response, Luke featuring 2 Live Crew's next album was titled **Banned In The USA**. Geffen Records refused to distribute

'90 Mill Vanilli collect a Grammy Award (but don't get to keep it).

The Geto Boys' new record because of the lyrical content of tracks like "Mind of a Lunatic," "Let a Ho Be a Ho," and "Trigga Happy Nigga," and Madonna was excoriated for simulating masturbation onstage during her "Blonde Ambition" tour.

Then there was the question of sampling; while Deee-Lite (whose "Groove Is In The Heart" was one of the year's slinkiest dance hits) and Public Enemy (who released *Fear Of A Black Planet*, their most uncompromising record yet) were among the many artists who sampled other people's records in a creative (and often unrecognizable) fashion, many others opted for a simpler approach, lifting the hooks wholesale from previous hits. Of this latter faction, **MC Hammer**'s "U Can't Touch This" and white rapper **Vanilla Ice**'s "Ice Ice Baby" were the most egregious, utilizing already familiar riffs from Rick James' "Super Freak" and Queen's "Under Pressure," respectively. Not coincidentally, they also became two of the year's biggest rap hits.

But the loudest howls of outrage were reserved for producer Frank Farian's revelation that Europop duo **Milli Vanilli**, who had recently won the Grammy Award for "Best New Artist," did not actually sing on their multi-platinum *Girl You Know It's True* LP. While the cheekbones and dance moves of "frontmen" Rob Pilatus and Fabrice Morvan certainly had as much to do with the album's sales as the bubblegum grooves within (anyone familiar with Boney M, Farian's late-seventies space-disco creations, should have suspected that all was not as it seemed), the National Academy of Recording Arts and Sciences stripped Pilatus and Morvan of their Grammy in November. The duo made another go of it a few years later, this time as Rob & Fab, but only sold a few thousand copies of their record. Pilatus' life became a downward spiral of drug and legal problems; in 1998, he died in a German hotel room from a mixture of pills and booze.

Wood OD's

Another victim of rock 'n' roll excess was Andrew Wood, lead singer of Seattle hard-rock band Mother Love Bone, who died of a heroin overdose shortly before his band's full-length debut was scheduled to be released. With heroin now cheaper, purer and more plentiful then it had been in decades, many observers predicted an marked increase in overdoses (and needle-related HIV cases) over the next few years.

TV News

Saturday Night Live, currently struggling through yet another uninspired season, created quite a hubub when it announced that controversial comedian Andrew Dice Clay would host an upcoming broadcast. As a protest against Dice's lewd and crude stand-up routines, cast member Nora Dunn boycotted the show, joined by scheduled musical guest Sinead O'Connor. A fresh (in several senses of the word) contrast to *SNL* was provided by **In Living Color**, Fox's new comedy-variety series; created by filmmaker Keenen Ivory Wayans, the show featured such memorable characters as "Homey the Clown" and the gay hosts of "Men on Film," as well as a talented young comedian named Jim Carrey. Fox also

IN THE NEWS

March 25 – After being ejected from the Happy Land Social Club in the Bronx, New York, Julio Gonzalez spills gasoline on the entrance and sets it on fire. The ensuing conflagration kills 87 people, and Gonzalez is given 25 years to life in prison.

April 22 – The 20th anniversary of Earth Day is celebrated worldwide, with 200 million people in 140 countries participating in tree planting, recycling, and other earth-friendly events.

June 30 – The National Academy of Science announces that the AIDS epidemic is not leveling off, but rather spreading to new groups, including black and Hispanic women.

July 26 – Bush signs a landmark law forbidding discrimination against disabled persons in employment, public accommodations, and transportation.

'90 Jim Carrey *(far right)* with the cast of *In Living Color*.

scored big with **The Simpsons**, the animated brainchild of "Life in Hell" comic artist Matt Groening. Bart Simpson, the show's troublemaking fourth-grader, immediately became an icon for underachievers of all ages, leading to a rapid proliferation of T-shirts bearing Bart's mantra, "Don't Have a Cow, Man." **Twin Peaks**, which also touched a nerve with viewers, was more of an acquired taste. Directed by David Lynch, the unsettling, dream-like serial revolved around the question of "Who killed Laura Palmer?" The plot became impossibly convoluted—and the ratings dropped severely—by the time detective Kyle Maclachlan got around to solving the mystery (answer: her dad, who became a homicidal maniac when possessed by an evil spirit named Bob), but the show further confirmed Lynch's reputation as a man with a darkly original vision, as well as making actress Sherilyn Fenn the sex symbol of the hour. Far more wholesome (though it regularly dealt with issues like drinking, drugs, and

'90 Doh! It's *The Simpsons*.

teen sex) was **Beverly Hills 90210**, an Aaron Spelling production that followed the lives of eight Beverly Hills high school students. The show became incredibly popular with teenage viewers, who tuned in religiously to catch the latest crisis, and the success of the series paved the way for such future Spelling favorites as *Melrose Place* and *Models Inc.*

Muppet Man Dies

On February 4, Eddie Murphy, Michael Jackson, Frank Sinatra, and Shirley MacLaine all appeared and performed as part of ABC's "Sammy Davis, Jr's Sixtieth Anniversary Celebration" special. The tribute came none too

soon, as Sammy died a few months later of throat cancer at the age of sixty-four. The country was further saddened by the sudden death (from pneumonia) of Jim Henson, creator of Kermit the Frog, Miss Piggy, and the rest of the Muppet gang. He was fifty-three.

Movie News

1990 saw the revision of the Motion Picture Association of America's rating system, which replaced X ratings with NC-17, meaning that no one under age seventeen would be admitted. *Henry and June*, Philip Kaufman's adaptation of Anais Nin's erotic diaries, was the first film to be classified NC-17 under the new system. The year's biggest hit,

however, was strictly PG—**Home Alone**, in which a young boy outwits a duo of burglars with an intricate series of booby traps, turned child star Macaulay Culkin into one of Hollywood's highest paid actors. *Teenage Mutant Ninja Turtles*, a live-action film based on the popular comic book, was another huge hit with kids, who gobbled up millions of dollars' worth of Ninja Turtle toys and costumes. Expecting a success of *Batman*-like proportions, a line of *Dick Tracy* memorabilia was marketed in well in

TOP ALBUMS

MC HAMMER
PLEASE HAMMER DON'T HURT 'EM

VANILLA ICE
To The Extreme

SINEAD O'CONNOR
I Do Not Want What I Haven't Got

PHIL COLLINS
...But Seriously

BONNIE RAITT
Nick of Time

advance of the movie's release. Unfortunately, reviews of the film (which starred Warren Beatty and Madonna) were mixed at best, and the merchandise collected dust on the shelves.

Arnold Schwarzenegger, who continued to alternate action roles and light-hearted comedy with *Total Recall* and *Kindergarten Cop*, was the year's most popular male star, while **Julia Roberts** (*Pretty Woman, Sleeping with the Enemy*) was the top female draw.

'90 Teenage Mutant Ninja Turtles.

'90 The ghost of a kiss for Demi Moore from Patrick Swayze.

Patrick Swayze romanced Demi Moore from beyond the grave in *Ghost*; Kevin Costner bonded with Native Americans in *Dances with Wolves*; and mob movie fans were offered the double treat of Martin Scorsese's *GoodFellas* and Francis Ford Coppola's *The Godfather, Part III*. Less enticing was *Ghost Dad*, starring Bill Cosby as a deceased parent continuing to raise his brood, and *Lambada* and *The Forbidden Dance*, both of which tried to exploit the current **Lambada** dance craze (although the former did feature the many talents of Adolpho "Shabba-Doo" Quinones, last seen in *Breakin' 2: Electric Boogaloo*). Worst of all was *Wild Orchid*, in which an orange-colored Mickey Rourke seduced real-life galpal Carre Otis during Carnival in Rio de Janeiro. Ostensibly an "erotic thriller" along the lines of Rourke's earlier *Nine and a Half Weeks*, the film was way too silly to be even remotely sexy.

Millions Netted

Though it had yet to become a household word, more and more Americans were logging onto the Internet. 1990 witnessed the introduction of America Online, which competed with the already established Prodigy and CompuServe networks by specializing in chat folders and offering an easy-to-use interface.

Videogame News

Nintendo rocked the videogame world with the release of Super Mario 3, which quickly became the best-selling game cartridge to date. Meanwhile, the company filed suit against Blockbuster Video, alleging that Blockbuster's rental of video-games severely dented Nintendo sales.

IN THE NEWS

August 2 – Under orders from Iraqi president Saddam Hussein, Iraqi troops invade Kuwait.

August 7 – The United States sends troops, armor, and aircraft to Saudi Arabia, in order to protect the country against a possible offensive by Iraqi troops.

August 10 – Twelve out of 21 member nations of the Arab League vote to support US and UN actions against Iraq.

November 5 – Bush signs a budget law intended to reduce the federal budget by $492 billion over the next five years. Despite Bush's famous "Read my lips: No new taxes" promise during the 1988 campaign, the law includes $140 billion in new taxes.

November 15 – Bush signs the Clean Air Act of 1990, which updates and tightens air pollution standards for the first time since 1977.

November 29 – The UN Security Council votes to authorize the US and its allies to use force to expel Iraq from Kuwait if Saddam Hussein does not withdraw his troops from the country by January 15, 1991.

Bud Dries Up

And just when you were wondering if technological wonders would never cease, the Anheuser-Busch Brewing Company introduced Bud Dry, which was specially brewed to have no bite or aftertaste. Unfortunately, the beer had no flavor, either, and poor sales caused it to be pulled off the market in 1994.

'91

As 1991 began, George Bush was riding high. Having spent months demonizing Saddam Hussein (Bush insisted on pronouncing the Iraqi leader's name as "Sodom," apparently for extra righteousness value) before the American public, the president was rewarded with a massive groundswell of popular support for the Gulf War.

TOP TELEVISION SHOWS

60 Minutes

Roseanne

Cheers

Murphy Brown

Home Improvement

ACADEMY AWARDS

BEST PICTURE

The Silence of the Lambs

directed by Jonathan Demme

BEST ACTOR

Anthony Hopkins

The Silence of the Lambs

BEST ACTRESS

Jodie Foster

The Silence of the Lambs

Though the war lasted barely a month and a half, Desert Storm Generals Norman Schwarzkopf and Colin Powell became household names, thanks to hourly televised updates of events in the Persian Gulf (Desert Storm trading cards helped the young 'uns keep abreast of the latest weaponry). By the end of February, Iraq was out of Kuwait, Bush was out from under Reagan's shadow (and almost assured of re-election in 1992), and America was "standing tall" again after successive humiliations in Vietnam and Iran.

Recession Deepens

But when the smoke finally cleared and the victory parades were over, things weren't quite so rosy. The recession, which had started the previous year, only seemed to be getting worse; unemployment was up to 7.2 percent, new home sales were down 5.6 percent, and new car sales were down 11.2 percent, giving Detroit its worst year since 1983. General Motors laid off seventy thousand workers, and

'91 Costner as DA Jim Garrison in *JFK*.

IBM axed another twenty thousand. In October, usually their busiest month, Las Vegas casinos reported severe drops in revenue, which in turn caused two of the city's gaming establishments to go bankrupt. In addition, studies revealed that 5.5 million American children were currently going hungry.

Movie News

It wasn't a particularly good year for Hollywood, either; whether it was because of the recession, or just due to the fact that everyone stayed home in January and February to watch the Gulf War on TV, theaters reported their lowest box-office attendance totals in twenty years. Certainly, 1991 didn't

lack for blockbusters—the hundred-million-dollar *Terminator 2: Judgment Day* was easily the year's most popular film, as Arnold Schwarzenegger continued to reign as Hollywood's pre-eminent action star. **Kevin Costner**, currently the most popular male box-office attraction, starred in *Robin Hood: Prince of Thieves* and Oliver Stone's controversial *JFK*. (Though many complained that *JFK* played fast and loose with the facts surrounding the Kennedy assassination, the inaccuracies were minor compared to those of Stone's *The Doors*, which was released the same year.)

Madonna's "Blonde Ambition" tour was documented in *Truth or Dare*, and Ice-T and Ice Cube delivered competent performances in *New Jack City* and *Boyz N the Hood*, respectively. But the hands-down winner of the "Worst Performance by a Popular Recording Artist" trophy had to be **Vanilla Ice**, who mumbled his way through the mind-numbingly stupid *Cool As Ice*. The surprise indie hit of the year was *Slacker*, Richard Linklater's plotless trawl through the

January 15 – The UN-authorized, US-led "Operation Desert Storm" begins in Kuwait with an all-out air attack.

January 25 – The AIDS death toll hits 100,000, with over 161,000 cases reported since 1981.

February 27 – After three days of ground offensive, Desert Storm troops rout the Iraqi forces in Kuwait. 146 American troops are killed in the fighting; 467 are wounded.

March 3 – After leading LA police on a car chase of several miles, black motorist Rodney King is arrested and severely beaten by four LAPD officers. The incident is captured on videotape by bystander George Holliday, and shown repeatedly on news programs across the country.

April 4 – The Environmental Protection Agency announces that the ozone layer over the US is being depleted at twice the rate previously thought.

April 16 – Seventy tornadoes touch down in seven states in the Midwest and Southwest, killing 23 people.

June 27 – Thurgood Marshall, the first black US Supreme Court justice, resigns after 24 years on the bench.

July 25 – Jeffrey Dahmer arrested in Milwaukee, Wisconsin for killing, dismembering, and possibly eating at least seventeen people. Dahmer confesses to the sex-related killings, and receives fifteen consecutive life sentences. In 1994, Dahmer is beaten to death in prison by a fellow inmate.

'91 Costner stars again, this time as *Robin Hood: Prince of Thieves*.

lives of idiosyncratic folks living in the college town of Austin, Texas. Alternately hilarious and annoying, the film launched Linklater's career as a director, and gave pop sociologists a handy new name for the post-Boomer generation.

Buddies Team Up On Film

In a year that saw the publication of such new-feminist best-sellers as Susan Faludi's *Backlash: The Undeclared War Against American Women* and Naomi Wolf's *The Beauty Myth*, 1991 fittingly offered numerous films with strong female characters. In **The Silence of the Lambs**, Jodie Foster played a tough FBI trainee tracking a serial killer with help from an imprisoned cannibal (Anthony Hopkins), while Mary Stuart Masterson helped Mary-Louise Parker stand up to an abusive husband in *Fried Green Tomatoes*. *Thelma and Louise*, starring Susan Sarandon and Geena Davis as two road buddies wanted for the murder of an attempted

rapist, inspired a popular T-shirt that sported a picture of the gun-toting pair and the legend, "George Bush— Meet Thelma and Louise!"

Of course, it was also the year that Robert Bly's **Iron John**: *A Book about Men* became the bible of the burgeoning "Men's Movement," and so there were also plenty of male-bonding films to go around. **Keanu Reeves** starred in no less than three "buddy" films, *Bill and Ted's Bogus Journey*, the goofy action-thriller *Point Break* (with Patrick Swayze), and Gus Van Sant's haunting *My Own Private Idaho*. The latter also starred River Phoenix, who received rave reviews for his portrayal of a narcoleptic street hustler.

TV News

Introduced briefly in 1990, *Northern Exposure*, a low-key comedy-drama about a young New York physician (Rob Morrow) assigned to a remote Alaskan village, became a smash in 1991 upon finally finding a permanent time slot. **Seinfeld**, a sitcom revolving around

stand-up comic Jerry Seinfeld and his three neurotic, self-involved friends (Jason Alexander, Julia Louis-Dreyfus, and Michael Richards), also inspired a devoted following, although it wouldn't really break through to the mainstream until 1993, when it was rescheduled to follow the phenomenally successful *Cheers*. The abrasive cartoon **Ren and Stimpy** was a smash with both children and young hipsters, who found the scatalogical humor and John Kricfalusi's eye-popping animation to be very much to their liking.

'91 **Seinfield and friends make their TV debut.**

Pee Wee Busted

Paul Reubens, aka Pee Wee Herman, made headlines in July when he was arrested for "exposing himself" in a Florida porno theater. In response, CBS quickly removed *Pee Wee's Playhouse* from its Saturday morning schedule, and Pee Wee Herman dolls disappeared overnight from the nation's toy stores, becoming instant collectables in the process. Clearly, Pee Wee should have stayed at home with his VCR, like most porno aficionados. In the triple-X world, "amateur porn" was now the latest fad, with over fifty different video companies buying and repackaging homemade sex tapes for sale or rent.

Videogame News

In other joystick news, Nintendo introduced its new Super NES system, which retailed for $249.95. Nintendo

'91 *Thelma and Louise*, **women on the run.**

TOP ALBUMS

GARTH BROOKS
Ropin' The Wind

MARIAH CAREY
Mariah Carey

NATALIE COLE
Unforgettable With Love

METALLICA
Metallica

MICHAEL JACKSON
Dangerous

was less than pleased with Galoob Toys, who introduced The Game Genie, a device which allowed players to cheat on Nintendo games and win more easily. Atari, still trying to recover from a disastrous second half of the eighties, announced the development of a new 16-bit system, which the company hoped would effectively compete with Sega and Nintendo; but with Sega's new **Sonic the Hedgehog** game setting sales records, Atari would have its work cut out for itself. Over at the arcade, business was picking up considerably, thanks to Capcom's new, ultra-violent Street Fighter II.

'91 Ren and Stimpy.

Music News

Michael Jackson became the world's highest-paid recording artist in March, when he signed a one-billion-dollar multimedia deal with Sony Software. He also came under fire for the video of his new single, "**Black Or White**," which featured him breaking windows; concerned parents worried that young fans might want to imitate his acts of destructiveness. Though Michael's new *Dangerous* CD sold six million copies, it was hardly the zeitgeist-defining success of *Thriller*; Garth Brooks, Mariah Carey, and Michael Bolton all sold more records than Michael in 1991.

Alternative Source Of Cash

Music lovers who didn't care for any of the above artists could at least take heart in the surprise success of Nirvana; *Bleach*, the Seattle band's previous album, was a college radio favorite, but **Nevermind**, their first record for Geffen Records, shot to the top of the charts, thanks in part to the anarchic video for "Smells Like Teen

Spirit." The success of *Nevermind*, REM's *Out of Time*, and the summer's Lollapalooza festival (which was founded by Jane's Addiction leader Perry Farrell, and featured appearances by The Rollins Band, Ice-T's Body Count, Siouxsie and the Banshees, The Butthole Surfers, and Nine Inch Nails) convinced record executives that "alternative rock" was where it was at. Major labels quickly swooped down on Seattle, signing any band in sight with guitars and flannel shirts; it seemed as if every time Nirvana leader **Kurt Cobain** praised an indie band in an interview, said band were immediately offered a multi-album deal.

As with previous industry feeding frenzies, the mediocre signings far outweighed the good ones, but it was obvious to observers that rock music was turning another corner; almost overnight, hair-metal bands—the music industry's bread-and-butter during the late-eighties—vanished completely from MTV. In their place, an army of "**grunge**" rockers (including Pearl Jam, Soundgarden, and Alice in Chains) expressed a vague dissatisfaction with their lot in life. It was progress, certainly, but it wasn't a whole lot of fun.

The Magic's Gone

In the NBA championships, Michael Jordan led the Chicago Bulls to a four-games-to-one victory over Magic Johnson and the Los Angeles Lakers. In November, Johnson shocked the sports world by suddenly announcing his retirement, due to the fact that he was HIV-positive. Johnson changed his mind and rejoined the team for the 1991–92 season, but retired again in November 1992.

1992 was, as George Bush so eloquently put it, "a weird year." For Bush, it began with a very public (and embarrassing) display of vomiting during a diplomatic visit to Japan, and ended with a resounding defeat at the hands of a man young enough to be his son. Certainly, Bush's re-election campaign was dogged by unforseen circumstances— the worsening recession, the LA riots, Texas billionaire H Ross Perot's third-party candidacy—but the president did little to help his own cause.

TOP TELEVISION SHOWS

60 Minutes
Roseanne
Murphy Brown
Home Improvement
Coach

ACADEMY AWARDS

BEST PICTURE
Unforgiven
directed by Clint Eastwood

BEST ACTOR
Al Pacino
Scent of a Woman

BEST ACTRESS
Emma Thompson
Howards End

Never the warmest of individuals, Bush sounded increasingly shrill and pinched as the campaign wore on and his approval ratings dipped; for all the controversy surrounding Democratic challenger Bill Clinton (he equivocated on several important issues, and was accused of carrying on at least one extramarital affair while presiding as the governor of Arkansas), Clinton at least came across like he cared about people. In the end, incidents like the takeover of the Republican Convention by Pat Robertson's **"Christian Coalition,"** and Bush's confusion during a staged question-and-answer session (he was visibly shaken when the order of questions was accidentally shuffled) only served to illustrate how deeply out of touch Bush was with the mood of the country. Americans showed their displeasure by making sure that Bush would go down in the history books as a one-term-only president.

'92 *Barney & Friends* became a merchandising bonanza.

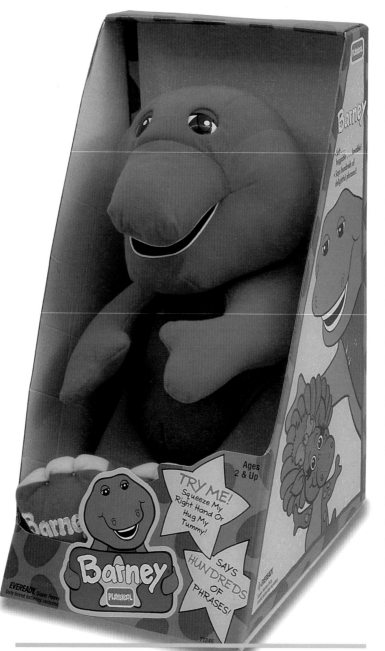

Clinton Plays It Cool

Among the more amusing missteps of the Bush/Quayle re-election campaign was Dan Quayle's blistering attack on Murphy Brown. In a May speech bemoaning America's "poverty of values," Quayle lit into the popular TV show, taking Candice Bergen's character to task for having a baby out of wedlock. The ensuing media hubub helped the show attain its highest ratings to date, while further diminishing the public's ability to take Quayle's seriously. Bill Clinton took a far more media-savvy (and friendly) approach, blowing saxophone (albeit terribly) as part of an appearance on *The Arsenio Hall Show*.

TV News

In retrospect, many parents would have been happier if Quayle had attacked *Barney & Friends,* the inane PBS children's show about a stuffed purple dinosaur who grows and comes to life. *Barney* quickly developed a devoted following among preschoolers, who of course petitioned their parents for stuffed purple dinosaurs of their own. By the end of 1993, over three hundred million dollars in Barney merchandise had been sold.

"Babewatch"

Had they been available, stuffed Pamela Anderson dolls would probably have been a big hit with men of all ages; as it was, male viewers had to be content with watching the buxom blonde actress (formerly *Home Improvement*'s "Tool Time Girl") run around in a red lifeguard's swimsuit on *Baywatch*. The show, which failed to capture a regular audience on its introduction in 1989, was now an international hit, thanks to the charms of such cast members as Anderson, Nicole Eggert, and Erika Eleniak.

Sitcoms And Talk Shows Come And Go

Melrose Place, Aaron Spelling's new dramatic series, also made good use of an attractive cast, including Heather Locklear, Josie Bissett, Courtney Thorne-Smith, Andrew Shue, and Grant Show. Some of the year's more popular sitcoms included *Love and War* (starring former Partridge Family member Susan Dey, replaced after one season by Annie Potts), *Mad About You* (with Paul Reiser and Helen Hunt), and *Martin* (featuring stand-up comedian Martin Lawrence), while *The Cosby Show*, the most popular sitcom of the last decade, ended its impressive run on April 30.

HBO's popular new *Larry Sanders Show* starred **Garry Shandling** as a neurotic talk-show host; the program's talk-show segments often included real-life guests like Sharon Stone and Elvis Costello, and were filmed in front

IN THE NEWS

April 29 – Rioting breaks out in Los Angeles, following an all-white jury's acquittal of the four LA policemen who were videotaped beating Rodney King. Three days of violence leave 51 people dead, 1,800 injured, and 3,767 buildings in ashes. On May 2, King holds a press conference, asking, "People, can we all get along?" LAPD Chief Daryl Gates is forced to retire in June, in part for withdrawing his men from LA's poorer neighborhoods at the start of the riots.

May 23 – With the USSR dissolved, President Bush signs an agreement with Russia, Belarus, Kazakhstan, and Ukraine to abide by the nuclear arms reduction treaty signed between the US and USSR in 1991.

June 22 – In the wake of the LA riots, Bush signs a bill providing $1.3 billion for relief to Los Angeles, and which will appropriate funds for a summer employment program in 75 cities.

June 23 – John Gotti, head of the Gambino crime family, is sentenced to life in prison for thirteen charges of murder, conspiracy, tax fraud, and obstruction of justice.

June 24 – The US Supreme Court rules that warning labels on cigarette packages do not protect tobacco companies from damage claims. The court also reaffirms its stance that state-sponsored prayer in public schools is unconstitutional.

June 29 – The US Supreme Court upholds women's constitutional right to abortion by a 5-4 vote, although the court does permit individual states to impose some restrictions.

'92 *Baywatch* **babes and hunks.**

of a live audience. Johnny Carson signed off from *The Tonight Show* in May, and was replaced by stand-up comedian Jay Leno. NBC's decision to hire Leno didn't sit well with David Letterman, who had also coveted the *Tonight Show* job, and industry insiders guessed that Letterman would soon take his sarcastic sense of humor to another network.

Denzel Washington plays Malcolm X.

Dumb And Dumber

If *The Hat Squad*, a short-lived crime series about three hunky vigilantes who wore fedoras, stood out as the year's dumbest show, it was hard to beat NBC's *Amy Fisher: My Story* for sheer real-life stupidity. The TV movie starred Noelle Parker as the "Long Island Lolita" who attempted to murder the wife of her lover, auto mechanic Joey Buttafuocco. In real life, Buttafuocco did six months for statutory rape, and became something of a minor celebrity (the tabloids gleefully reported that he'd been kicked out of an exclusive Manhattan swinger's club for eating a pastrami sandwich in the communal hot tub), while Fisher was sentenced to five to fifteen years in jail.

Movie News

Movie attendance was still down in 1992, but controversy was way up. Spike Lee got in trouble for recommending that black kids skip school to see his new **Malcolm X**, starring Denzel Washington; gay and feminist activists picketed *Basic Instinct*, protesting Sharon Stone's role as a rapacious bisexual murderess; and Ernest Dickerson's *Juice* (starring Tupac Shakur), Abel Ferrara's *The Bad Lieutenant* (with Harvey Keitel as a *really* bad lieutenant), and **Reservoir Dogs** (Quentin Tarantino's acclaimed directorial debut) all came under fire for their extreme violence.

Party On!

Home Alone 2: Lost in New York and Disney's animated *Aladdin* were huge hits with the kids, as was the eighty-million-dollar *Batman Returns,* which featured Danny DeVito as The Penguin and Michelle Pfeiffer as Catwoman. Younger viewers also flocked to see **Wayne's World**, a film adaptation of Mike Myers' and Dana Carvey's regular *Saturday Night Live* sketch; the film's soundtrack, which featured such classic rock gems as Queen's "Bohemian Rhapsody" and Gary Wright's "Dream Weaver," topped the charts for several weeks. Other popular soundtracks included *Boomerang* (featuring Boyz II Men, Babyface, and Toni Braxton), *Singles* (with tracks by Seattle bands Mudhoney, Pearl Jam, and Soundgarden), and Whitney Houston's soundtrack to **The Bodyguard**, which sold over fifteen million copies.

Music News

In music, 1992 was the year where juvenile rappers Kriss Kross had kids wearing their clothes backwards, Billy Ray Cyrus started a line-dancing revival with "Achy Breaky Heart," and Prince signed a one-hundred-million-dollar recording contract with Warner Brothers. Madonna released *Erotica,* the aural companion to *Sex,* her controversial photo book, and Body Count, Ice-T's speed-metal band,

TOP ALBUMS

WHITNEY HOUSTON
The Bodyguard

BILLY RAY CYRUS
Some Gave All

GARTH BROOKS
The Chase

DEF LEPPARD
Adrenalize

NIRVANA
Nevermind

platform with an elastic cord tied to your ankles. Though scary, the sport was surprisingly safe; only two bungee-related deaths were reported during the year.

'92 The US boasted over 200 bungee-jump sites in 1992.

IN THE NEWS

July 15–16 – The Democratic National Convention nominates Arkansas Governor Bill Clinton and Tennessee Senator Al Gore for president and vice-president.

August 19–20 – The Republican National Convention nominates President Bush and Vice-President Quayle for re-election.

August 23 – Secretary of State James Baker resigns his post in order to take over Bush's re-election campaign, which is widely seen to be in serious trouble.

August 24 – Hurricane Andrew hits southern Florida; the hurricane's 150 mph winds kill 38, destroy 85,000 homes, and leave 250,000 homeless.

September 24 – Following an inquiry into allegations of sexual harassment at the US Navy's 1991 Tailhook Convention in Las Vegas, two Navy admirals are forced to retire, and a third is reassigned.

November 3 – Bill Clinton is elected president by a margin of 5 million votes. Third-party candidate H Ross Perot logs a surprising 19 percent of the vote.

December 24 – Outgoing President Bush pardons six former federal officials, including former secretary of defense Caspar Weinberger and former national security advisor Robert McFarlane, for their roles in the Iran-Contra scandal.

caused a stir with a track called "Cop Killer;" under pressure from the White House, Time-Warner stockholders and various right-wing organizations, Sire Records eventually dropped Ice-T from their roster. Lollapalooza had a prosperous second year, thanks to an all-star lineup consisting of the Red Hot Chili Peppers (currently riding high with "Under the Bridge"), Ice Cube, Pearl Jam, Lush, The Jesus and Mary Chain, Soundgarden, and Ministry. The **HORDE** ("Horizons of Rock Developing Everywhere") Tour was a successful "hippie" alternative to Lollapalooza, featuring such jam-happy acts as Blues Traveler, the Spin Doctors, Phish, Widespread Panic, The Aquarium Rescue Unit, Bela Fleck and the Flecktones.

Car Industry Bullish

Though the economy was still hurting, Detroit bounced back impressively, with automobile sales up twenty-one percent from the previous year. Ford's Taurus was the year's top-selling American car, moving over three hundred and ninety-seven thousand units, and sales would rise even higher during the next two years. While the dependable Taurus appealed to the conservative impulses of American auto buyers, Dodge's new **Viper**, a voluptuously styled sports car that could go 0 to 60 in 4.5 seconds, was all about sex and speed. Though it was priced at fifty thousand dollars, demand for the car far out-stripped the supply.

18–30s Targeted

Observing the runaway success of alternative rock, marketers increasingly geared their advertising campaigns towards eighteen-to-thirty-year-olds, the "Generation X" demographic (usually by featuring young guys with goatees and big shorts in their commercials), and tried hard to give their products an "alternative" spin, whether or not they actually warranted one. **Zima**, the Coors Company's new "clear malt beverage" was a typical example—the alcoholic brew was marketed as a cool alternative to beer, even though its sweet taste was more appealing to the wine-cooler crowd. **Adidas**, a company that connected easily with the eighteen-to-thirties, responded to a sudden demand for old three-striped styles by reactivating its Gazelle and "shell-toe" lines.

They Fell For It!

In an effort to help the public (and advertisers) more fully understand those mysterious Gen-Xers, *The New York Times* published a glossary of "grunge" terminology in its November 15 issue. Unfortunately for the *Times*, the glossary turned out to be a hoax, perpetrated by Megan Jasper of New York indie label Caroline Records. In retrospect, it's hard to believe that there wasn't anyone at the paper hip enough to know that "swingin' on the flippity-flop" was *not* slacker slang for "hanging out."

Nor was it grunge lingo for **bungee jumping**, which was all the rage at the time. For fifty dollars you could jump from an elevated

'93

nineteen

"Drugs don't work," announced the Partnership for a Drug-Free America's new ad campaign, but the truth of the matter was that, for many, drugs were working just fine—a University of Michigan study showed that pot use among teens was up for the first time in thirteen years. Marijuana chic was everywhere, from the cover of Dr Dre's *The Chronic* to the popular pot-leaf insignias sported on T-shirts and baseball caps.

TOP TELEVISION SHOWS

60 Minutes
Roseanne
Home Improvement
Seinfeld
Murder, She Wrote

ACADEMY AWARDS

BEST PICTURE
Schindler's List
directed by Steven Spielberg

BEST ACTOR
Tom Hanks
Philadelphia

BEST ACTRESS
Holly Hunter
The Piano

A drug-induced heart attack put an end to River Phoenix's promising film career, but his very public death (on Halloween, outside the entrance to LA's Viper Room) did little to diminish the hip cachet of hard drugs in film and music circles. In other addictive substance news, Anheuser-Busch proudly announced that their new **Budweiser Ice Draft** had a smoother taste than regular beer, but it's likely that more people bought it for the increased alcoholic content.

Bad Behavior

In Ohio, a woman claimed that MTV's new *Beavis and Butthead* cartoon caused her five-year-old son to set the fire that torched their trailer park home and killed his two-year-old sister. In LA, rapper Snoop Doggy Dogg was arrested by the Los Angeles Police Department in connection with a drive-by shooting; just across town, the LAPD was investigating allegations that Michael Jackson had molested a twelve-year-old boy. (Beavis and Butthead would have

enjoyed Jackson's televised denial, if only because the "**King of Pop**" actually used the word "penis" in his prepared statement.) Also of note in the City of Angels, "Hollywood Madam" Heidi Fleiss was arrested for running a high-priced call-girl ring (actor Charlie Sheen was known to be one of her many showbiz-related clients), and brothers Erik and Lyle Menendez admitted to the brutal shotgun slaying of their parents, a crime which had gone unsolved for nearly four years. After years of abuse at the hands of her husband, housewife Lorena Bobbitt fought back by chopping off his penis while he slept. Doctors were able to reattach the severed member, thus enabling **John Wayne Bobbitt** to find fame in the best-selling porno videos *John Wayne Bobbitt: Uncut* and the appropriately titled *Frankenpenis*. On the big screen, Woody Allen's *Manhattan Murder Mystery* stalled at the box office, due to the lingering controversy over his relationship with

'93 Wanted: Snoop Doggy Dogg.

Soon-Yi Previn, adopted daughter of Allen's long-time girlfriend Mia Farrow.

Painful Pranks

Mortal Kombat, the year's most popular videogame, included a "finishing moves" feature that allowed you to rip the heart out of your opponent; parental groups were, predictably, less than thrilled. Nor were they particularly happy to see **body-piercing** become a nationwide fad, thanks in part to Alicia Silverstone's navel-piercing scene in Aerosmith's "Cryin'" video. The youth of America was further corrupted (and inspired) by The Jerky Boys, three New Yorkers who sold thousands of copies of a CD consisting solely of obnoxious prank phone calls.

"Girls And Boys Come Out..."

"Lesbian Chic—the Bold, Brave New World of Gay Women," trumpeted *New York* magazine's May issue, which featured singer kd lang on the cover. Public acceptance of "alternative lifestyles" was hardly widespread, however; it was all right for entertainers like lang or Melissa Etheridge to come out of the closet, but—thanks to the military's confusing new "**don't ask, don't tell**" policy—gays were allowed to enlist in the armed forces only so long as they didn't identify themselves as such. And the Mattel Toy company was clearly embarrassed when their Earring Magic Ken doll became the best-selling Ken doll of all time; clad in a purple mesh top and sporting a familiar-looking ring on a necklace, the doll was much more popular with gay men than with little girls.

TV News

The big news in TV land was that, after eleven years on NBC, David Letterman signed a contract with CBS for sixteen million dollars. That amount was strictly small potatoes compared to the sales of Mighty Morphin Power Rangers merchandise; within months of the show's debut, American toy stores had sold over three hundred and fifty million dollars' worth of Power Rangers toys and gear. *The X-Files* made its debut in September to relatively little fanfare, but the adventures of agents Mulder (David Duchovny) and Scully (Gillian Anderson) quickly built a cult following before the year was out. Also debuting was *Star Trek: Deep Space Nine*, a spin-off of *Star Trek: The*

TOP SINGLES

Mariah Carey
"Dreamlover"

Janet Jackson
"That's The Way Love Goes"

UB40
"Can't Help Falling in Love"

Snow
"Informer"

Meat Loaf
"I'd Do Anything For Love (But I Won't Do That)"

'93 "I'm listening." Frasier (Kelsey Grammer) on the couch with Eddie

Next Generation. Lois and Clark: The New Adventures of Superman made stars out of previously obscure actors Dean Cain and Teri Hatcher, while *NYPD Blue* made producer **Steven Bochco** a household name, thanks to controversy over the show's steamy content. Among the year's popular new sitcoms were *The Nanny*, starring Fran Drescher (previously best-known for her role as Bobbie Fleckman in *This Is Spinal Tap*); *Grace Under Fire*, starring Brett Butler; *Frasier*, a *Cheers* spin-off starring Kelsey Grammer; and *These Friends of Mine*, which was later renamed *Ellen* after its star, comedienne Ellen Degeneres. 1993 brought more variations on the **Amy Fisher/Joey Buttofuco** saga—ABC offered *The Amy Fisher Story*, starring the recently rehabbed Drew Barrymore, while CBS weighed in with *Casualties of Love: The Long Island Lolita Story*, starring former *Who's the Boss?* nymphette Alyssa Milano. In the top-rated special of the 92–93 season, Oprah Winfrey

interviewed Michael Jackson for ABC; Jackson amused viewers by admitting to having had a "minor" amount of plastic surgery. Talk-radio DJ Howard Stern closed out 1993 with a pay-per-view New Year's special; featuring an army of scantily clad female extras, the program scored the highest all-time rating for a pay-per-view special.

One of Stern's favorite guests, busty Guess jeans model **Anna Nicole Smith**, was the hot babe of the moment, thanks to being crowned *Playboy*'s "Playmate of the Year" and topping the charts with a best-selling video. Though she would star in the following year's *Naked Gun 33⅓: The Final Insult*, Smith's acting career never really got off the ground, although she did make headlines a few years later by marrying ninety-year-old billionaire oil tycoon J Howard Marshall.

The Naked And The Dead

In Hollywood, it was a year of extremes. Steven Spielberg's dinosaur

thriller **Jurassic Park** grossed a record three hundred and fifty million dollars at the box office, while Arnold Schwarzenegger's *Last Action Hero* was an unexpected flop. Films like *Philadelphia*, *Schindler's List*, and *The Piano* were box-office successes despite their serious themes, while *Indecent Proposal* (in which Robert Redford offered Woody Harrelson a million dollars to sleep with Demi

'93 Hot playmate Anna Nicole Smith.

Moore) succeeded in spite of its ludicrous premise. Tim Burton's *The Nightmare Before Christmas* received rave reviews for its special effects, yet they were no match for the stunning visuals of **The Crow**. Already dark in theme and design, the film gained additional weight (and drawing power) from the death of star Brandon Lee (son of Bruce), who was accidentally shot by a prop gun near

TOP ALBUMS

Mariah Carey
Music Box

Janet Jackson
Janet

Pearl Jam
Vs

Garth Brooks
In Pieces

Eric Clapton
Unplugged

'93 Spielberg's *Jurassic Park* was a monster hit at the box office.

the end of the production. **Tom Hanks** starred in the romantic comedy *Sleepless in Seattle,* and won an Oscar for his performance as a dying AIDS patient in *Philadelphia.* Richard Linklater didn't win any Oscars for *Dazed and Confused,* his semi-nostalgic look at high school life in the mid-seventies, but the film did introduce future stars Parker Posey, Ben Affleck and Matthew McConaughey to the movie-going public.

'93 Liam Neeson and Ben Kingsley in *Schindler's List.*

Music News

In April, the American music industry finally did away with the 6- by 12-inch cardboard longbox it had been using for CD packaging. It was not missed. Greatly mourned, however, was the passing of **Frank Zappa**. The idiosyncratic composer died of prostate cancer on December 4th; it is possible he hastened off this mortal coil to escape the new country craze that saw Garth Brooks sell five million copies of *In Pieces* and Brooks and Dunn sell three million of *Hard Workin' Man.*

Gangsta Rap did exceptionally well in 1993, thanks to albums like Dr Dre's *The Chronic,* Cypress Hill's *Black Sunday,* Snoop Doggy Dogg's *Doggy Style,* and Ice Cube's *Lethal Injection.* Janet Jackson dipped back into the sound of old-school soul for her new *Janet* CD, and Rupaul (born Rupaul Andre Charles) became the highest-charting transvestite in history with the club smash, "Supermodel (You Better Work)." Grunge rock, still a year or two away at this point from complete self-parody, carved out out a pretty decent market share of its own. Produced by Steve Albini for maximum sonic discomfort, Nirvana's *In Utero* debuted at the top of the charts in October, while Pearl Jam's *Vs* did the same in November, despite the band's marked refusal to do videos. Regular video play helped The Stone Temple Pilots' *Core* sell three million copies, ditto for The Smashing Pumpkins' three-million-selling *Siamese Dream.*

Alternative Airwaves

Indeed, alternative rock was quickly becoming as mainstream as the music it purported to be an alternative to. AAA radio ("Adult Album Alternative") was born in late 1993 on San Francisco's KFOG-FM and Seattle's KMTT-FM. The format, which mixed mildly alternative rock tracks with inoffensive classic rock, was an immediate success among slightly older, slightly less hip individuals. Meanwhile, designer Marc Jacobs integrated "the grunge look" into his Perry Ellis collection, and Anna Sui and Isaac Mizrahi co-opted the "baby doll" fashions popularized by Hole singer Courtney Love and Babes in Toyland leader Kat Bjelland.

Bullseye!

In sports, Cincinnati Reds owner Marge Schott received a year's suspension from baseball for making racist and anti-Semitic remarks about her players. In basketball, the Chicago Bulls won the NBA championship for the third straight year, beating the the the Phoenix Suns four games to two. Michael Jordan, who'd led the league in scoring for seven out of his nine seasons, announced his retirement shortly afterwards, but would return to lead the Bulls to the championship in 1996 and 1997.

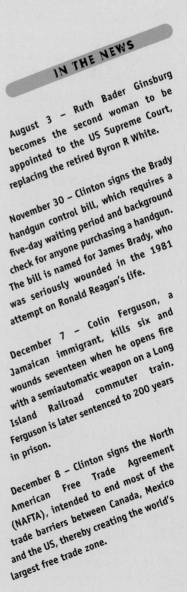

IN THE NEWS

August 3 – Ruth Bader Ginsburg becomes the second woman to be appointed to the US Supreme Court, replacing the retired Byron R White.

November 30 – Clinton signs the Brady handgun control bill, which requires a five-day waiting period and background check for anyone purchasing a handgun. The bill is named for James Brady, who was seriously wounded in the 1981 attempt on Ronald Reagan's life.

December 7 – Colin Ferguson, a Jamaican immigrant, kills six and wounds seventeen when he opens fire with a semiautomatic weapon on a Long Island Railroad commuter train. Ferguson is later sentenced to 200 years in prison.

December 8 – Clinton signs the North American Free Trade Agreement (NAFTA), intended to end most of the trade barriers between Canada, Mexico and the US, thereby creating the world's largest free trade zone.

The American tabloid press, long vilified by adherents of "real" journalism, received a serious credibility boost in 1994, thanks to the scandals surrounding Michael Jackson and OJ Simpson. In both cases, the *National Enquirer*, the *Star*, and the *Globe* all regularly broke stories well ahead of the other, more conventional media outlets.

TOP TELEVISION SHOWS

Seinfeld

Home Improvement

60 Minutes

Grace Under Fire

ER

ACADEMY AWARDS

BEST PICTURE

Forrest Gump

directed by Robert Zemeckis

BEST ACTOR

Tom Hanks

Forrest Gump

BEST ACTRESS

Jessica Lange

Blue Sky

There was plenty of grist for the tabloid mills, of course; in January, Jackson agreed to settle out of court with the twelve-year-old boy who'd brought a sexual abuse case against him. Though Jackson continued to proclaim his innocence, the settlement was believed to be worth over fifteen million dollars. In August, the boy's stepfather filed a lawsuit against Jackson, alleging that the singer had used his power and influence to try to ruin the boy's family; the suit was thrown out in September, when the boy refused to testify against Jackson in court. Jackson's life took an even more bizarre turn in March, when he married **Lisa Marie Presley**, daughter of Elvis, in a civil ceremony in the Dominican Republic. Rumors about the munion abounded (Was Michael after Lisa Marie's inheritance? Was she trying to convert him to Scientology? Would he help her land a recording

'94 LAPD picture of OJ Simpson, taken following his arrest on suspicion of murdering his ex-wife and her male companion.

contract?), but mostly it seemed like a calculated ploy to help shore up Michael's crumbling reputation.

Did He Do It?

OJ Simpson's reputation was quite another matter. With his smooth manner and good looks, the former football star was extremely popular as an actor, pitchman, and sports commentator; when his ex-wife Nicole and her male acquaintance Ron Goldman were brutally murdered on the night of June 12, it seemed unthinkable that OJ could have been involved. But as evidenced mounted against him, the LA police department decided on June 17 that it had no choice but to make an arrest. By then, unfortunately, OJ had disappeared; when the police finally tracked him down, he was holding a gun to his own head in the back of a white Ford Bronco, driven by former teammate Al "AC" Cowlings. As television viewers across the country looked on, Cowlings led police on a bizarre slow-speed car chase back to Simpson's abode, where Simpson was arrested. Police found his passport and ten thousand dollars in cash in the vehicle.

Vice On Ice

In another strange-but-true incident, figure skater Tonya Harding and three others (including Harding's husband) pleaded guilty of conspiracy to assault Nancy Kerrigan, Harding's rival in the Lillehammer Olympic games. Kerrigan had been attacked by a "mystery assailant" on January 6, five weeks before the games were to begin; though her leg had been injured in the attack, she still skated away with the silver medal. Harding came in eighth, but achieved immortality of a different sort when the X-rated home video of her wedding night became an oft-bootlegged VCR favorite.

Americans Approve Rough Justice

In May, American teenager Michael Fay found his fifteen minutes of fame after being arrested in Singapore for spray-painting parked cars. Though the Clinton administration tried to intervene, Fay received the country's standard punishment for the crime—four strokes on the backside with a wet rattan cane. Rather than protest the caning, most Americans seemed to be in favor of it; with a recent study showing a 154-percent increase since the mid-eighties in violent crimes committed by young men between ages fifteen and nineteen, many suggested that the US would benefit from meting out similar punishments to youthful offenders.

TV News

Many television viewers only had eyes for the neverending jury selection process of the OJ trial, which was televised live from the courtroom by day and subjected to continual analysis on evening news programs. Despite this, many new shows were able to thrive. Hospital dramas *ER* (*above*), which turned George Clooney into a popular heartthrob, and *Chicago Hope* found a devoted audience, as did the syndicated sci-fi show *Babylon 5* and the gritty crime series *New York Undercover*. **Friends**, which revolved around six young and attractive New Yorkers, was the year's most popular sitcom; as the US Bureau of Labor estimated that twenty percent of American graduates now held jobs that didn't require a college degree, the show's over-educated, under-achieving characters struck a chord with twentysomething viewers. The "**Rachel**," named for Jennifer Aniston's character on the show, became the most popular women's hairstyle of the mid-decade. Less popular, though highly acclaimed, were *South Central* (a comedy-drama about a single-parent black family living in Los Angeles), *My So-Called Life* (starring Claire Danes as a smart-but-confused teen), and *Party of Five*, a dramatic series about five children (including Matthew Fox and Neve Campbell) trying to carry on in the

IN THE NEWS

January 17 – A massive earthquake strikes Los Angeles, killing 51, injuring over 5,000, and leaving 15,000 homeless. The temblor, registering somewhere between 6.6 and 6.8 on the Richter Scale, causes at least $15 billion in damage.

May 26 – Clinton signs a law protecting abortion clinics, making it a federal crime to attack or blockade clinics, their operators, or their patrons.

August 5 – Former Reagan and Bush official Kenneth Starr replaces Robert Fiske, Jr as the independent counsel for the continuing Whitewater investigation.

October 21 – The US and North Korea sign an agreement to freeze North Korea's nuclear reactor program.

'94 Close *Friends.*

wake of their parents' deaths. Of the three, only *Party of Five* managed to last more than a season on the air. *Beverly Hills 90210* remained as popular as ever, but it went into the fall season without **Shannon Doherty**; the volatile actress, whose tantrums and drinking binges were the stuff of legend, left the show for greener pastures in the spring.

Music News

Shannon Doherty and Lisa "Left Eye" Lopes probably would have made one hell of a team; Lopes, of the popular rap trio TLC, made headlines in June by burning down the mansion of her boyfriend, Atlanta Falcons wide receiver Andre Rison, in a drunken rage. Rison was forgiving, as were courts, which only sentenced Lopes to five years' probation.

Without question, the saddest news of the year was that of **Kurt Cobain**'s suicide. Always uncomfortable with his degree of celebrity (to say nothing of the media's attempts to brand him as a "spokesman for his generation"), the Nirvana leader had been plagued throughout his short career by depression and a heroin problem, and the mounting pressures of the music business simply became too great for him. After disappearing from an LA rehab clinic where he was supposed to be detoxing, Cobain went back to his home in Seattle and blew his head off with a shotgun. **Hole**, featuring Courtney Love, Cobain's widow, released the ironically titled *Live Through This* shortly thereafter.

Red-Hot Lineups At Festivals

With the disparate likes of A Tribe Called Quest, The Beastie Boys, The Smashing Pumpkins, The Breeders, Nick Cave, George Clinton and The P-Funk Allstars, Green Day, The Verve, and The Boredoms on hand (as well as Stereolab, Guided By Voices, The Pharcyde, and Luscious Jackson playing the second stage), Lollapalooza featured its strongest lineup to date. Green Day, whose multi-platinum *Dookie* CD showed that there was indeed room for punk rock in the mainstream, also put on an impressive, mud-caked performance at **Woodstock '94**, the twenty-fifth anniversary concert event that featured sets by Nine Inch Nails, Soundgarden, Porno for Pyros, and the Red Hot Chili Peppers, as well as old-timers like Santana and Crosby, Stills and Nash. This time around, the love beads and moccasins were replaced by **Doc Martins** (*below*) and navel, nipple, nose, and eyelid piercings, ecstacy was substituted for LSD, and the organizers weren't letting anyone in for free; tickets were available at a hundred and thirty-five dollars apiece for a block of four, or two hundred dollars apiece for individual admission.

Easier Listening

Henry Mancini, composer of the themes for *Peter Gunn*, *The Pink Panther*, *Charade*, and countless other film and TV projects, died June 14 at the age of seventy. Sadly, he passed away just as his music was starting to be appreciated by a new generation of listeners. Lounge and easy-listening sounds of the fifties and sixties were back in style, thanks to the release of *I, Swinger*, the debut record by cocktail revivalists Combustible Edison, and **Space Age Bachelor Pad Music**, Bar/None Records' new compilation of hard-to-find Esquivel tracks. Many listeners found these whimsical records to be a refreshing antidote to the dull grind of grunge; soon, venerable labels like RCA and Capitol were raiding their own vaults for long-lost classics of the Rat Pack era.

Movie News

You couldn't go anywhere in 1994 without hearing the songs from Disney's new animated musical, *The Lion King*, just as it was simply impossible to get away from people riffing on the "Life is like a box of chocolates" line from *Forrest Gump*. Thankfully, there was also Quentin Tarantino's **Pulp Fiction**, which featured dialogue so amusing ("You know what they call a Quarter Pounder in Amsterdam? A Royale with Cheese!") and a soundtrack so cool (featuring such 1960s surf classics as Dick Dale's "Misirlou" and The Centurions' "Bullwinkle, Pt 2") that you didn't mind hearing them replayed. John Travolta, mired for years in *Look Who's Talking* purgatory, proved that he could still do great work, but

it was Samuel L Jackson—as the Bible-quoting hitman—who really stole the show. Oliver Stone also added to the year's violence quotient with the bloody *Natural Born Killers*.

Jim Carrey, who came on like a mutant version of Jerry Lewis, scored big box-office hits with *Ace Ventura, Pet Detective, Dumb and Dumber*, and *The Mask*. Tim Allen also made the transition from small screen to large with the popular holiday entry, *The Santa Clause*, but the year's funniest film was probably Kevin Smith's **Clerks**, a comedy about a couple of foul-mouthed guys working at a convenience store and video shop. Shot in black-and-white on a budget of twenty-seven thousand dollars, *Clerks* proved (once again) that you didn't need special effects or big-name stars to get a hit. Of course, it didn't hurt, either; *True Lies* (Arnold Schwarzenegger's latest) and *Speed* (with Keanu Reeves and Sandra Bullock) both lured in millions with a combination of big-budget explosions

'94 Forrest Gump meets JFK.

its judging procedures, but the changes came too late to help *Hoop Dreams*.

Not Excused

In a class-action lawsuit against silicone breast implant manufacturers, sixty companies were ordered to pay a total of 4.25 billion dollars to 90,500 women who claimed to have been injured by their implants. Luckily, Sara Lee's uplifting Wonderbra debuted in 1994, thus diminishing the need for implants, at least for women outside of the sex industry. In related news, **supermodels** Elle McPherson, Naomi Campbell and Claudia Schiffer opened the Fashion Café in New York City. Though she'd recently made fifty thousand dollars modeling a pair of black jeans for No Excuses

and high-profile stars. ***Interview with the Vampire: The Vampire Chronicles*** may not have had any explosions, but it did have Brad Pitt and Tom Cruise—though Anne Rice fans were appalled at the very thought of having Cruise portray their beloved Lestat. Even more appalling was the fact that ***Hoop Dreams***, an excellent film charting four years in the lives of two young inner-city basketball players and

their families, was completely passed over for a "Best Documentary" Oscar nomination. The ensuing outcry caused the Academy to re-examine

jeans ad, Paula Jones—the former Arkansas government worker currently suing President Clinton for sexual harassment—was not invited to the opening.

'94 *Left: Natural Born Killers—Woody Harrelson and Juliette Lewis, and (inset) an uneasy association with food? Supermodels McPherson, Campbell, and Schiffer.*

TOP ALBUMS

The Lion King
soundtrack

BOYZ II MEN
II

PINK FLOYD
The Division Bell

STONE TEMPLE PILOTS
Purple

KENNY G
Miracles: The Holiday Album

On January 25, opening statements began in the case of *The People of the State of California v Orenthal James Simpson*, better known as "the trial of the century." With television crews allowed into the courtroom by LA Superior Court Judge Lance Ito, the trial quickly became a circus; everyone, from Simpson lawyer Johnnie Cochran to Judge Ito himself, seemed to be playing to the cameras.

TOP TELEVISION SHOWS

Seinfeld
ER
Home Improvement
Friends
60 Minutes

ACADEMY AWARDS

BEST PICTURE
Braveheart
directed by Mel Gibson

BEST ACTO
Nicholas Cage
Leaving Las Vegas

BEST ACTRESS
Susan Sarandon
Dead Man Walking

Prosecutors Marcia Clark and Christopher Darden painted a picture of Simpson as a control freak who had previously stalked and beaten Nicole, while Simpson's "dream team" of Cochran, Robert Shapiro, and F Lee Bailey argued that their client was the innocent victim of either the sheer incompetence of the LA police department, or a massive conspiracy masterminded by racist LAPD officer Mark Fuhrman.

Polls showed that American opinions about the case were split along racial lines, with the majority of blacks believing OJ to be innocent, and most whites judging him guilty; in Los Angeles, where the police department and the criminal justice system had long given minorities the shaft, this disparity was even more pronounced. Despite compelling evidence pointing to Simpson's guilt, few were truly surprised when, on October 3, he was **acquitted** by the jury of nine blacks, two whites, and one latino after only four hours of deliberation.

During the trial and its aftermath, fame smiled briefly on many of those

'95 Trial by television—OJ Simpson in court.

involved with the case. Over thirty books about the trial were published in 1995, including the autobiography of Brian "**Kato**" Kaelin, OJ's hunky houseguest. Kato parlayed his newfound celebrity into unsuccessful gigs as a stand-up comic and talk-radio host, while Al "AC" Cowlings began appearing at autograph conventions in the company of the white Bronco. Paula Barbieri, who

had broken off a relationship with OJ on the night of the murders, took the place of soft-porn star Shannon Tweed in the straight-to-video *Night Eyes* series. Prism Pictures, who produced the series, further played up the OJ connection by putting a figure with a black ski mask and long knife (both of which Simpson was alleged to have used in the murders) on the video box.

That's THEIRstory...

With Michael Jackson's two-CD set of old and new material, the modestly titled *HIStory: Past, Present And Future—Book 1*, due for a July release, Jackson and wife Lisa Marie appeared on *ABC's Primetime Live* in June to do some advance promotion. Viewers hoping to see Jackson answer some pointed questions about the recent sexual molestation allegations were sorely disappointed, as an obviously awestruck Diane Sawyer only lobbed the softest possible queries in Michael's direction. Though the couple did their best to act affectionately towards each other, it was hardly a convincing performance; Michael tried to flash a studly grin when Lisa Marie offered an unprompted, "**Do we have sex?** Yes, yes, yes!", but no one seemed especially surprised when the pair divorced seven months later.

Music News

What was especially surprising in 1995 was the runaway success of Hootie and The Blowfish's *Cracked Rear View*,

which was still selling like hot cakes a year after its initial release. Though the music itself was basically just drab bar-band rock, something about the singles "Hold My Hand," "Let Her Cry," and "Only Wanna Be With You" struck a chord with the American public, who scarfed up over fourteen million copies of the album. Also striking an unexpected nerve was Canadian singer-songwriter **Alanis Morissette**, who moved over eleven million copies of her American debut, *Jagged Little Pill*. Although there was nothing new about Morissette's off-pitch singing style or her liberal use of four-letter expletives (Chicago singer-songwriter Liz Phair had recently racked up critical raves for the same shtick), her angry-young-woman attitude immediately won her a dedicated legion of followers.

After years without an actual home, the **Rock and Roll Hall of Fame** finally opened in Cleveland, housed in a new, ninety-two-million-dollar structure designed by award-winning architect IM Pei. The Hall's opening ceremonies featured concert performances by Chuck Berry, Little Richard, The Kinks, Bruce Springsteen, and **Sheryl Crow**, who was currently high in the charts with *Tuesday Night Music Club*. This year's Lollapalooza festival featured Hole, Sonic Youth, Pavement, Beck, Jesus Lizard, the Mighty Mighty Bosstones, Sinead O' Connor (who had to split early due to pregnancy), and Cypress Hill, although it was obvious that most of the attendees were just there to display their tattoos and piercings or surf the mosh pit, regardless of who happened to be onstage at the time.

'95 Alanis Morissette.

More Musicians Leave The Stage

Latina singer Selena (full name: Selena Quintanilla) was on the verge of crossover success when she was shot to death, on March 31, by the founder of her fan club. Months later, her commercial breakthrough came in the form of *Dreaming Of You*, her first English-language recording. **Tupac Shakur**, having recently survived a murder attempt, received a jail sentence in February in connection with a 1993 sexual assault. Released while the rapper was in prison (he was out on parole by the year's end), the aptly titled *Me Against The World* became Tupac's best-selling record to date. Former NWA rapper **Eazy-E** (Eric Wright) died on March 26th of AIDS, now the leading killer of Americans aged twenty-four to forty-four; his last album, *Str8 Off Tha Streetz Of Muthaphukkin Compton*, would top the charts the following year, leaving such sentimental musings as "Hit The Hooker" and "Nutz On Ya Chin" to remember him by. Other passings in the music world included the overdose death of Shannon Hoon, lead singer of Blind Melon, and Dean Martin, who went to the great lounge in the sky at the age of seventy-eight. **Jerry Garcia**, who had been plagued by drug problems for the last two decades, died in a rehab clinic at the age of fifty-three, effectively bringing the long, strange trip of the Grateful Dead to an end.

Movie News

In 1995, Hollywood offered a little something for everyone. At any given multiplex, you could find moving dramas (*Leaving Las Vegas*, *Dead Man Walking*, *Apollo 13*) nestled cheek-by-jowl with witty comedies (*Get Shorty*, *To Die For*), nostalgic rehashes (*The Little Rascals*, *The Brady Bunch Movie*), dumb farces with *Saturday Night Live* alums, trashy Tarantino knock-offs (*Things to Do In Denver When You're Dead*; *From Dusk Till Dawn*, which actually featured Tarantino in a supporting role), and just plain trash (*Showgirls*).

Kevin Costner's post-apocalyptic *Waterworld* was a $235-million flop, while **Batman Forever** (starring Val Kilmer as the caped crusader, and Jim Carrey as The Riddler) raked in $184 million at the box office, making it the year's biggest film. Kids of all ages went to see *Toy Story*, *Pocahontas*, and *Babe*, but no one under the age of eighteen could get in to see *Kids*, Larry Clark's controversial look at a bunch of amoral high schoolers; Alicia Silverstone's **Clueless** character, on the other hand, preferred to get her kicks from shopping instead of unsafe sex and illicit drug use.

Demi Moore took off her clothes again in *The Scarlet Letter*; Whitney Houston, currently married to troubled singer Bobby Brown, sounded all too convincing complaining about the lack of decent men in her life in *Waiting to Exhale*; and Sharon Stone's ludicrously drawn-out death scene almost sank Martin Scorsese's otherwise excellent *Casino*.

Surfing for Thrills

With Americans logging onto the Internet in record numbers, it wasn't at all surprising to see a handful of **"techno-thrillers"** pop up in theaters in 1995. Unfortunately for Hollywood, most folks preferred to stay home and surf the Net than go see stinkers like *Hackers*, *Johnny Mnemonic* (with Keanu Reeves), and *The Net* (starring Sandra Bullock).

Bad Connections

Attempting a hard-hitting exposé about pornography on the Internet, *Time* magazine's panic-stricken **"Cyber Porn"** cover story only succeeded in increasing the amount of one-handed net-surfing going on

'95 *Toy Story* characters.

TOP SINGLES

COOLIO
"Gangsta's Paradise"

TLC
"Waterfalls"

TLC
"Creep"

SEAL
"Kiss From A Rose"

MARIAH CAREY
"Fantasy"

TOP ALBUMS

HOOTIE AND THE BLOWFISH
Cracked Rear View

GARTH BROOKS
The Hits

BOYZ II MEN
II

THE EAGLES
Hell Freezes Over

TLC
Crazysexycool

across the country. When Nebraska Senator Jim Exon proposed the so-called Communications Decency Act as a way to ban porn from the net, online companies responded by offering Adult Check and other filtering products to keep minors from viewing X-rated websites. Sales were slow for videogames in 1995, perhaps because of the increased interest (prurient or otherwise) in the Internet. The most popular game system by far was Sony's new **PlayStation**, which offered a hefty amount of quality titles, and retailed for around $299.

TV News

TV Talk Shows—Have They Gone Too Far? That was the topic on the table in March, when the "Secret Admirers" segment of the **Jenny Jones** show ended in tragedy. After learning on the show that his secret admirer was a man, enraged guest Jonathan Schmitz allegedly drove to the house of his secret admirer and killed him. It sounded like a future case for **Murder One**, Steven Bocho's acclaimed new crime series, which took the novel approach of following the

progression of a single murder case over the entire season. Other popular shows included *The Drew Carey Show*, *The Single Guy*, and *Caroline In the City* (sitcoms which took their cues from *Seinfeld* and *Friends*), *Star Trek: Voyager* (the first regular series aired on the new UPN network), and *Cybill*, Cybill Shepherd's new sitcom. The surprise hits of the year were *Hercules—The Legendary Journeys* and *Xena: Warrior Princess*, both of which mixed **swords-'n'-sorcery**

scenarios with knowing humor and attractive leads; in no time, *Hercules'* Kevin Sorbo and *Xena's* Lucy Lawless were two of America's more popular pin-ups.

Café Society

As Starbucks continued to spread the gospel of gourmet coffee, coffee bars were now the most popular places for young professionals to hang out. Cybercafés, where you could order a cup of joe while surfing the Net and arguing the merits of Microsoft's new Windows 95, were also increasing in number. As a result of the recent cigar boom—sales of premium cigars were up twenty-nine percent over the past three years—cigar bars started to pop up in urban areas. Usually, though, cigar aficionados had to go to special "cigar nights" at restaurants or bars in order to socialize and smoke with other stogie fanciers. The fad wasn't limited to men, either; studies showed that women now made up five percent of the cigar-chomping populace.

'95 Middle-aged fun in *Cybill*.

IN THE NEWS

December 31 – The federal government shuts down in a dispute between President Clinton and the Republican-controlled Congress over balancing the budget. Over 260,000 federal employees are furloughed for two weeks, and many public services are halted. House speaker Newt Gingrich and his fellow Republicans engineered the shutdown in an attempt to embarrass Clinton, but the plan backfires when the public blames Congress for the impasse.

'95 Star Trek's *Voyager*.

'95 Pin-up princess Lucy Lawless

1996 saw Bill Clinton become the first Democratic president since Franklin Roosevelt to be elected to two full terms. For the most part, his victory was something of a foregone conclusion; the economy remained in good shape, and his opponent, long-serving Republican senator Bob Dole, couldn't seem to come up with a platform more compelling than that it was *his* turn to be president.

TOP TELEVISION SHOWS

ER

Seinfeld

Friends

Suddenly Susan

Home Improvement

ACADEMY AWARDS

BEST PICTURE

The English Patient

directed by Anthony Minghella

BEST ACTOR

Geoffrey Rush

Shine

BEST ACTRESS

Frances McDormand

Fargo

Dole's major gaffes on the campaign trail—which included lambasting death-metal bands who hadn't existed for at least a decade, falling off a podium in Chico, California, and claiming on national television that tobacco was not, in fact, addictive—were compounded by his austere mein and the fact that he was over two decades older than Clinton.

After some hemming and hawing, H Ross Perot ran again as a third-party candidate, but his showing was less impressive this time around; although Perot did manage to wangle 7.8 million votes (three hundred thousand more than Clinton's margin of victory over Dole), it was less than half the total he received in 1992.

Primary Colors, a scabrous, anonymously written "novel" about Clinton's presidential campaign, was one of the year's best-selling books. After months of speculation, the author's identity was revealed to be that of Joe Klein, a conservative *Newsweek* columnist who'd previously denied authorship.

Gore-geous!

Clinton's secret re-election weapon, of course, was that he had a vice-president who could do the macarena at any time or place. The dance—sort of an advanced hokey-pokey—was currently sweeping the country, erupting seemingly whenever a large group of people were gathered, and VP Al Gore's repeated willingness to throw some macarena shapes couldn't help but reflect positively on the Clinton/Gore campaign.

Music News

Ska and swing were two other musical crazes beginning to infiltrate the mass consciousness. While the former remained primarily a club phenomenon and had yet to penetrate the charts, LA's ska-poppers **No Doubt** managed to sell several million copies of their *Tragic Kingdom* CD; though the band's sound was hardly authentic bluebeat (and though "Don't Speak," their smash power ballad, sounded like a slowed-down version of Irene Cara's "Fame"),

'96 **"Don't cry for me, Argentina..." Madonna as Evita.**

their success inspired a frenzied major label trawl for other ska acts. Gwen Stefani, No Doubt's Madonna-esque frontperson, was romantically linked with Gavin Rossdale of Bush, a British grunge band whose *Sixteen Stone* album proved far more popular in the states than in their homeland. **Snoop Doggy Dogg** (real name: Calvin Broadus) had two reasons to celebrate in 1996; not only was he back in the charts with *The Doggfather*, his second album, but he was also finally acquitted of murder charges stemming from a 1993 shooting. Tupac Shakur wasn't so lucky; his two records, *All Eyez On Me* and *Don Killuminati: The 7 Day Theory* (released under the name Makaveli) charted well, but he died from wounds received in a September 13 shooting in Las Vegas. To date, the crime hasn't been solved. The year's other popular rap records included Bone Thugs-N-Harmony's *E1999 Eternal* and Lil' Kim's *Hard Core*. **Beck** (full name: Beck Hansen), who had first attracted

'96 **Mega-bucks sci-fi movie** *Independence Day*.

'96 The Solomons come down to Earth in *Third Rock from the Sun*.

attention with 1994's "Loser," proved that his previous hit was no fluke; *Odelay*, an innovative mixture of breakbeats, samples, and general weirdness, was voted "Album of the Year" in countless critics' polls.

Radio Rivals

The US government's Telecommunications Act of 1996 lifted limits on the number of radio stations big businesses could purchase; as a result, commercial radio became increasingly generic. Alanis Morissette continued to dominate the "commercial alternative" stations, but she had some serious competition in the form of **Fiona Apple** and **Jewel**. The former's *Tidal* was an angry, brooding record featuring songs like "Shadowboxer" and "Criminal," while the latter's *Pieces Of Me* was filled with sweet pop-folk numbers like "You Were Meant For Me." Most likely, neither were in attendance when the original members of **Kiss** slapped on the old

TOP SINGLES

Los Del Rio
"Macarena (Bayside Boys Mix)"

Mariah Carey and Boyz II Men
"One Sweet Day"

Celine Dion
"Because You Loved Me"

The Tony Rich Project
"Nobody Knows"

Mariah Carey
"Always Be My Baby"

makeup and reunited to pillage the nation's enormo-domes. The group was in fine, filthy form, and the reunion tour grossed over forty-four million dollars.

Movie News

Widely touted as "the year of the independent film," 1996 did indeed have more than its fair share of low-budget successes. Jon Favreau's *Swingers* took an amusing look at young hipsters in LA, and made a star out of Vince Vaughn; Billy Bob Thornton's *Sling Blade* won an Oscar for "Best Screenplay Adaptation," Todd Solondz's *Welcome to the Dollhouse* won praise for its unflinching portrayal of the horrors of adolescence, and Joel and Ethan Coen had the biggest hit of their careers with **Fargo**, a droll crime story starring Frances McDormand as a pregnant Minnesota police chief. But when all was said and done, it was still the big-budget flicks that brought home the bacon. **Independence Day** (essentially a nineties update of the cheesy flying-

saucer films of the fifties) and **Twister**, two of the year's highest-grossing films, were short on substance but boasted eye-popping special effects. *Space Jam*, in which Michael Jordan helped Bugs Bunny and Porky Pig defeat an alien basketball team, fared extremely well at the box office, as did *Evita*, starring Madonna. Woody Harrelson and Courtney Love gave impressive performances as the *Hustler* publisher and his junkie wife in Milos Forman's *The People Versus Larry Flynt*. Eddie Murphy regained some commercial momentum with his remake of *The Nutty Professor*, Honk Kong action star Jackie Chan finally had his first American hit with *Rumble in the Bronx*, and Wes Craven had his biggest hit since *Nightmare on Elm Street* with *Scream*, featuring Neve Campbell as a teenager menaced by a killer obsessed with horror films. *Jerry Maguire* starred Tom Cruise as a struggling sports agent, but it was fellow actor Cuba Gooding's Oscar-winning supporting performance that had all of America shouting, **"Show me the money!"**

IN THE NEWS

March 13 – The Liggett Group, the smallest of the nation's five major tobacco companies, shocks the tobacco industry by settling a class action lawsuit over the detrimental health effects of smoking.

April 3 – US Secretary of Commerce Ronald H Brown perishes, along with 34 others, when his military plane crashes into a mountain in Dubrovnik, Croatia. The same day, Theodore J Kaczynski, a 53-year-old loner, is arrested and charged with being the so-called Unabomber.

June 13 – After an 81-day standoff, sixteen members of the Freemen, a right-wing extremist group, surrender to federal officials in Montana. Fourteen members are charged with threatening federal officers and defrauding banks and businesses of more than $1.8 million.

June 25 – A truck bomb kills nineteen American soldiers and wounds 300 people in Dhahran, Saudi Arabia. No suspects are apprehended.

Un-bare-able

Some of the year's major losers included *Barb Wire*, Pamela Anderson Lee's disastrous screen debut; *Kazaam*, starring basketball star Shaquille O'Neal as a friendly genie "owned" by an obnoxious little white boy; *Grace of My Heart*, Alison Anders' botched look at pop music in the Brill Building era; and **Striptease**, Demi Moore's unbelievably awful comedy-drama about a young mother who has to strip to raise funds for an upcoming child-custody hearing. The latter triggered some unintentional political hilarity when Bob Dole, desperately digging for a relevant issue on the campaign trail, condemned Moore for baring all in the film. Bruce Willis, Moore's husband (and a prominent supporter of the Republican party), suggested that the candidate mind his own damn business, and an embarrassed Dole quickly apologized.

TV News

In February, responding to widespread viewer criticism about the violent content of prime-time TV programs, the four major networks announced an agreement to establish a rating system for television shows. By the end of the year, they proposed a plan to rate programs "TV-Y" (suitable for all children) to "TV-M" (mature audiences only), but many critics complained that the system was not specific enough.

Some of the year's most popular new shows included **Third Rock From the Sun**, starring John Lithgow and Jane Curtin as space aliens trying to blend into the American suburbs, and

Just Shoot Me, starring David Spade as Laura San Giacomo's blisteringly sarcastic secretary. The biggest small-screen surprise had to be *Suddenly Susan*, which proved, after years of awful film appearances, that Brooke Shields actually had something of a flair for comedy.

Centenarian Dies

George Burns, one of early TV's most popular comedians (and one of the first TV stars to "break the fourth wall" by speaking directly to the camera) died on March 9th after a long and distinguished career. He was a hundred.

Fat Chance

1996 brought good news for weight-conscious snackers, when the Food and Drug Administration approved the use of Olestra, a fat substitute, for snack foods such as potato chips; the fact that many people reported experiencing stomach cramps and "anal leakage" after ingesting Olestra products didn't seem to bother anyone at the FDA. McDonald's introduced the **Arch Deluxe**, a sandwich aimed at the adult demographic, but it flopped; adults, it seemed, preferred the less "sophisticated" pleasures of a Big Mac. The home fitness business continued to boom, perhaps spurred by studies showing that Americans were more obese than ever. Marketed in slightly variant versions by several different infomercials, the AbRoller was the year's most popular piece of home-exercise equipment.

'96 Tickle Me Elmo, the "must-have" toy of '96.

Centenary Edition Hits The Road

1996 witnessed the passing of the American auto industry's one-hundredth anniversary, which Plymouth celebrated in fine style by producing the limited-edition Prowler roadster. With its small cockpit and retro styling, the aluminum-skeletoned two-seater agreeably harkened back to the custom hot rods of the forties and fifties.

Playing With Danger

If Tyco's giggling Tickle Me Elmo doll was the year's hottest Christmas toy, Cabbage Patch Snacktime Kids were the most controversial. In nearly one hundred separate incidents, the dolls—which had a mechanism enabling it to "eat" plastic carrots and french fries—actually chewed the hair and fingers of children feeding it. Eidos Interactive's **Tomb Raider**, a 3-D adventure game starring buxom cyber-heroine Lara Croft (*Newsweek* called her "the perfect fantasy girl for the digital generation"), became one of the year's most popular computer games.

TOP ALBUMS

ALANIS MORISSETTE
Jagged Little Pill

MARIAH CAREY
Daydream

CELINE DION
Falling Into You

Waiting to Exhale
soundtrack

FUGEES
The Score

July 17 – A TWA Boeing 747 jet explodes over the Atlantic Ocean shortly after takeoff from New York's Kennedy International Airport, killing all 230 people aboard. Theories about the blast blame mechanical failure, terrorist action, or accidental downing by a missile from a nearby military base, but findings remain inconclusive.

July 27 – A bomb explodes in a park in Atlanta, Georgia, during Summer Olympics festivities, killing one and injuring 100. Security guard Richard Jewell is briefly held as a suspect, then released; he later files defamation suits against the FBI and various media outlets.

September 26 – Astronaut Shannon Lucid sets an American record for time in space after spending 188 days aboard Russia's MIR space station.

November 5 – Clinton is re-elected president.

December 5 – Clinton appoints Madeline Albright, US representative to the UN, to be his new Secretary of State. She becomes the first woman ever to hold the post.

December 18 – The Oakland CA school board passes a resolution to treat black English, or "ebonics," as a second language. Controversy predictably ensues.

December 26 – The body of six-year-old beauty pageant contestant JonBenet Ramsey is found dead in the basement of her Boulder, Colorado, home. Her death is originally thought to be the result of a bungled kidnapping, but when her wealthy parents John and Patsy refuse to cooperate with the investigation, speculation increases that they were somehow involved, and that local police have bungled crucial evidence in the case.

As 1997 began, people across the country began to make plans to celebrate an important milestone in American pop culture—the fiftieth anniversary of the crash of an alleged flying saucer in Roswell, New Mexico. Though few people were aware of the incident fifty years ago, word of it had since spread to such an extent that "Roswell" was now virtually synonymous (at least among UFO buffs) with "government cover-up."

TOP TELEVISION SHOWS

ER
Seinfeld
Veronica's Closet
Friends
Touched By An Angel

ACADEMY AWARDS

BEST PICTURE

Titanic
directed by James Cameron

BEST ACTOR

Jack Nicholson
As Good As It Gets

BEST ACTRESS

Helen Hunt
As Good As It Gets

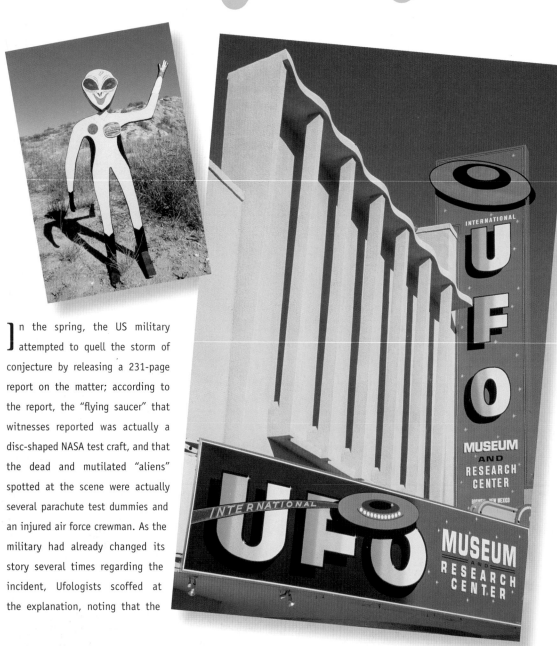

In the spring, the US military attempted to quell the storm of conjecture by releasing a 231-page report on the matter; according to the report, the "flying saucer" that witnesses reported was actually a disc-shaped NASA test craft, and that the dead and mutilated "aliens" spotted at the scene were actually several parachute test dummies and an injured air force crewman. As the military had already changed its story several times regarding the incident, Ufologists scoffed at the explanation, noting that the military did not even use parachute test dummies back in 1947. The truth, as *X-Files* fans were fond of saying, was still out there.

Star Comes Out

1997 also marked the fiftieth anniversary of the birth of commercial television; appropriately enough, it was the liveliest TV year in recent memory. *Ellen*'s **Ellen DeGeneres** caused a stir with her decision to come out of the closet, but that was nothing compared to the furore surrounding the decision to have her character come out as well. Thirty-six million viewers tuned in on April 30 to watch Ellen kiss guest star Laura Dern; fearing a boycott by conservative Christians, Wendy's, Chrysler, and JC Penney all pulled their ads from the broadcast. DeGeneres' very public relationship with actress Anne Heche was also a source of criticism from both straights and gays; the two were photographed hanging all over each other at a White House function, which many folks felt was in poor taste.

'97 **The one where Ellen comes out...**

Others called Heche's sincerity into question—she and Ellen had made their relationship public just days before Heche's new *Volcano* hit the multiplexes—and felt her admission that she'd "been straight before I met Ellen" only reinforced the image of homosexuals as predatory creatures.

Albert Crosses The Line

Not that heterosexuals were any less predatory, of course. In September, NBC sportscaster Marv Albert lost his job after pleading guilty to charges of sodomy and assault and battery, stemming from an incident that involved him savagely biting a female acquaintance in a hotel room. Albert had originally denied all charges, but when further revelations came to light

regarding Albert's alleged bisexuality and penchant for wearing garter belts and ladies lingerie, the toupeed announcer finally had no choice but to throw in the towel.

Dry Humor

New hits were few and far between in 1997. *Veronica's Closet*, featuring Kirstie Alley as a former fashion model, and *Dharma and Greg*, starring newcomer Jenna Elfman as a hippie who impulsively marries a yuppie, were the year's biggest new sitcoms; *Jenny*, a comedy variety show starring obnoxious former *Playboy* playmate/*MTV Singled Out* hostess Jenny McCarthy, was one of the year's biggest flops, despite reviews hyping McCarthy as "the next Lucille Ball."

Public opinion was sharply divided on *Ally McBeal*, a comedy-drama starring Calista Flockhart (*right*) as a

yuppie lawyer with a hyperactive imagination; the show inspired a fanatic following, but many of the unconverted thought the title character was pathetic and in desperate need of a life. Not so with *Buffy the Vampire Slayer*, played by Sarah Michelle Gellar; the poor girl was so occupied with staving off the undead, she barely had time to worry about her social life.

Over-Exposed

In an attempt to boost its TV ratings, which had sagged considerably over the past few years, contestants in the seventy-seventh Annual Miss America Pageant were allowed to wear two-piece swimsuits, and sport navel rings and tattoos. You could see most of the above—and a whole lot

more—in the Pamela Anderson and Tommy Lee video currently being sold on the Internet. Allegedly stolen from a locked safe in their home, the video depicted the happy couple swimming nude, having sex, rolling joints, and uttering endless inanities.

Blue Brew

It did not, however, show either of them drinking Motley Brue, a beverage manufactured by the Skeleteens soda company in honor of the reunited Motley Crue's new *Generation Swine* CD. In addition to a tangy ginseng-and-jalapeno flavor, the soda boasted the added attraction of turning your feces blue.

Music News

According to the music industry, 1997 was supposed to be the year that electronica became "the next big thing." **Electronic music** was enthusiastically supported by the country's music press, and MTV (which these days rarely played videos for more than an hour at a time) actually devoted a weekly program to ambient

TOP SINGLES

ELTON JOHN
"Candle In The Wind 1997"

JEWEL
"You Were Meant For Me"

PUFF DADDY AND FAITH EVANS
"I'll Be Missing You"

TONI BRAXTON
"Unbreak My Heart"

PUFF DADDY
"Can't Nobody Hold Me Down"

and electronica videos, but—with the exception of England's Prodigy—electronica failed to succeed outside of the rave/dance-club circuit. Part of the problem was radio, which was offering less and less support to music outside the parameters of "commercial alternative." The airwaves were jammed with one-hit wonders like OMC ("How Bizarre"), Sugar Ray ("Fly"), Smash Mouth ("Walking On The Sun"), Meredith Brooks ("Bitch"), Squirrel Nut Zippers ("Hell"), and teeny "MMMBop"-ers Hanson. Rap radio was dominated by Sean **"Puff Daddy"** Coombs (*above*), crowned "The New King of Hip-Hop" by *Rolling Stone* after the March 9 death by shooting of his friend and colleague Christopher Wallace, aka Notorious BIG.

Religious Unrest

Thanks to the success of *Antichrist Superstar*, Marilyn Manson (real name: Brian Warner) could lay uncontested claim to the title of "the Alice Cooper of the nineties." And, as with Alice before him, the rumors about the goings-on at his shows were far more bizarre than anything he actually got up to. According to the right-wing Christians who picketed his shows, Marilyn regularly slaughtered animals onstage, passed out drugs to the audience, and engaged in public sex with nine-year-old boys.

The religious right were no more tolerant of their own kind—after **Pat Boone** appeared at the American Music Awards dressed in leather and

wearing studded wristbands and fake tattoos (a publicity stunt to promote his new album of heavy metal covers), the Trinity Broadcast Network promptly Boone's *Gospel America* TV show.

Girls Make It On Their Own

Lilith Fair, a traveling festival made up entirely of female acts, was the surprise hit of the summer. Organized by Canadian singer-songwriter Sarah McLachlan, the tour featured sets by Jewel, Paula Cole, Tracy Chapman, Suzanne Vega, the Indigo Girls, and others, and proved to the previously skeptical music industry that an all-girl bill could be successful.

Titanic Sinks Also-Rans

Five months late and way over budget, James Cameron's *Titanic* confounded the cynical expectations of industry odds makers by becoming the top-grossing film of all time. Not even *The Lost World* (Steven Spielberg's follow-up to *Jurassic Park*) or *The Men in Black* (an enormously popular sci-fi comedy starring Will Smith) were any match for the commercial onslaught of Cameron's film, nor for the outpouring of love and worship heaped by fans upon *Titanic* star **Leonardo DiCaprio**.

1997 was, in many ways, a year of comebacks. Jim Carrey bounced back from the relative failure of 1996's *The Cable Guy* with *Liar, Liar*, and 1970s blaxploitation goddess Pam Grier scored her most high-profile role in years as the star of Quentin Tarantino's *Jackie Brown*. Sylvester Stallone and Kim Basinger racked up raves for their respective performances in *Cop Land* and *LA Confidential*, with

LEONARDO DiCAPRIO
KATE WINSLET
NOTHING ON EARTH
COULD COME BETWEEN THEM.
A JAMES CAMERON FILM
TITANIC
FROM THE DIRECTOR OF 'ALIENS,' 'T2' AND 'TRUE LIES'
TWENTIETH CENTURY FOX AND PARAMOUNT PICTURES PRESENT A LIGHTSTORM ENTERTAINMENT PRODUCTION A JAMES CAMERON FILM "TITANIC" LEONARDO DiCAPRIO KATE WINSLET BILLY ZANE
KATHY BATES FRANCES FISHER BERNARD HILL JONATHAN HYDE DANNY NUCCI DAVID WARNER AND BILL PAXTON RANDY GERSTON JAMES HORNER DEBORAH L. SCOTT
AL GIDDINGS GRANT HILL SHARON MANN JAMES CAMERON RICHARD A. HARRIS CONRAD BUFF, A.C.E. PETER LAMONT RUSSELL CARPENTER, A.S.C. DIGITAL DOMAIN
RAE SANCHINI JAMES CAMERON AND JON LANDAU JAMES CAMERON
LIGHTSTORM

Basinger even winning a "Best Supporting Actress" Oscar for her role in the neo-*noir* thriller. But the biggest comeback of all belonged to **Burt Reynolds**. Hoping for a break the previous year, he'd taken the role of the perverted congressman in *Striptease* for a cut-rate fee. When that movie stiffed, things looked especially bleak—until Burt's performance in *Boogie Nights* (as the porn director who gave Mark "Marky-Mark" Wahlberg his big break) won him a "Best Supporting Actor" Oscar nomination.

There were other highlights, as well: Mike Myers spoofed James Bond films of the sixties with *Austin Powers*, a crusty Jack Nicholson romanced waitress Helen Hunt in *As Good As It Gets*, Jennifer Lopez sizzled as *Selena*, Howard Stern played himself in *Private Parts*, and Ben Affleck and Matt Damon made hearts flutter in *Good Will Hunting*.

Farley Follows His Hero

The dire action-comedy *Beverly Hills Ninja*, briefly a hit in the theaters, was sadly notable only for the fact that it was the last Chris Farley vehicle released while he was still alive. An obese, eager-to-please comic with a flair for physical comedy, Farley adhered too closely to the hard-living aesthetic of his hero, John Belushi, and so it came as no surprise when he died of a drug-related heart attack in December. Like Belushi, he was thirty-three at the time of his death.

Kids Demand Care-ful Designs

Already hugely popular in Japan, Bandai's Tamagotchis, or "virtual pets," were all the rage in the US in 1997. Retailing for between $9.99 and $12.99, the little electronic buggers (which required you to take care of their needs by pushing specific buttons, lest they "die" from neglect) were moving out of New York's FAO Schwarz at a rate of around eighty thousand a week. Smelling a good thing, the Tiger Electronics and Playmates companies released respective knock-off versions known as Giga Pets and Nanos. Educators, parents and sociologists were all wondering the same thing: Are Tamagotchis teaching kids responsibility, or are they just stressing them out?

Mattel brought Barbie into the computer age with Talk with Me Barbie, who came with a little computer and a CD-Rom that enabled the doll to talk to you. The company also introduced **Becky**, Barbie's disabled pal (who came with a pink and purple wheelchair), and teamed up with MasterCard to launch Cool Shoppin' Barbie, who came complete with a tiny MasterCard and a credit card scanner.

'97 Pam Grier as Jackie Brown.

TOP ALBUMS

The Spice Girls
Spice

No Doubt
Tragic Kingdom

Celine Dion
Falling Into You

Space Jam
soundtrack

Jewel
Pieces Of You

June — Tobacco companies agree to pay $368 billion to states to defray smoking-related health care costs. All human images and characters are banned from cigarette advertising.

July 4 — The *Mars Pathfinder* probe, launched December 4, 1996, lands on Mars and sends back pictures of rocky landscape. Argument rages over whether or not to send humans next time.

July 15 — Italian designer Gianni Versace is gunned down on the steps of his Miami Beach residence by gay serial killer Andrew Cunanan, who kills himself in a nearby houseboat a few days later. Cunanan was being sought by the FBI in connection with four other murders.

August — Microsoft's Bill Gates buys $150 million worth of shares in Apple Computers. Apple stock rises 33 percent after the announcement, but experts are divided about the potential long-term effect on the company and the computer market.

November — Saddam Hussein expels US arms inspectors from Iraq. Suspecting that the Iraqi leader is continuing to manufacture chemical weapons, Clinton weighs whether or not to attack him. Hussein eventually backs down and lets the inspectors get on with their business.

'97 Bandai's Tamagotchis— toys to cherish?

Hate crimes against gays and lesbians were up across the country, according to statistics, and the "El Niño" weather system caused the wettest US winter on record—but this was nothing compared to the storm clouds that hung over the White House during 1998. Saddam Hussein threatened several times over the course of the year to halt all UN inspections of Iraqi weapons facilities, demanding an end to the US's damaging economic sanctions against his country.

TOP TELEVISION SHOWS

ER

Seinfeld

Friends

Touched By An Angel

Veronica's Closet

ACADEMY AWARDS

BEST PICTURE

Shakespeare in Love

directed by John Madden

BEST ACTOR

Roberto Benigni

Life Is Beautiful

BEST ACTRESS

Gwyneth Paltrow

Shakespeare in Love

'98 Clinton puts his credibility on the line.

With Americans split over whether to use force against Saddam (and further split over how *much* force to use), the US failed to form a coherent strategy for dealing with the situation, opting for the occasional bombing run (or threat thereof) each time Saddam Hussein ejected weapons inspectors.

But the biggest bomb dropped on the home front: Having spent some forty million dollars trying to prove that Bill and Hillary Clinton were somehow involved in the convoluted Whitewater real estate scandal, independent counsel Kenneth Starr suddenly expanded his inquiry to include an investigation into allegations that President Clinton had had an affair with White House intern **Monica Lewinsky**, and that the President had coerced her into lying about it to investigators. Clinton stated several times that he "never had sex with that woman," but finally admitted to having a relationship with

Lewinsky after evidence to that effect proved insurmountable. He did, however, continue to insist that his statements had been "legally accurate," drawing a hair-splitting distinction between oral sex and actual fornication.

An Upstanding Man

As far as the media seemed to be concerned, everything else going on in the world paled in importance next to "Zippergate" or "Monicagate," as the scandal was variously known. It became virtually impossible to turn on the TV or open a newspaper without seeing a picture of Lewinsky, hearing some titillating new detail about the case, or being subjected to someone's opinion about the seriousness of the charges against the President. Some commentators called for his immediate resignation—or, failing that, his impeachment; others condemned Starr for conducting a "**sexual witch-hunt**" with taxpayers' money, likening him to Joe McCarthy. (For his part, Starr preferred to think of himself as Joe Friday from *Dragnet*.) About the only thing anyone seemed to agree upon was that Linda Tripp (the government employee and "friend" of Lewinsky's, who had surreptitiously taped their discussions of the intern's affair with Clinton) was a vindictive and generally repulsive person. Meanwhile, parents across the country wrung their hands over how exactly to answer their children's persistent questions about oral sex, while stand-up comics alternated Lewinsky jokes with cracks about **Viagra**, the popular new anti-impotence drug currently being endorsed by Bob Dole.

In September, Starr's exhaustive

report on the matter was released to the media, and million of people from around the world logged on to read it from various websites. And yet, for all of Starr's findings and allegations, Clinton's approval polls remained remarkably high. The robust health of the country's economy didn't hurt, to be sure, nor did his role in brokering the Wye River peace accord between the PLO and Israel.

Though poll after poll showed that the majority of Americans wished to "move on," the US House of Representatives voted in October to open **impeachment** hearings. Voters responded to the Republican Party's increasingly shrill and self-righteous anti-Clinton tirades by handing Republican candidates a series of surprise defeats in the November elections; hours later, House speaker Newt Gingrich resigned from his post. (In another election-day surprise, former pro wrestler Jesse "The Body" Ventura won the race for governor of Minnesota.)

The Republicans continued to press on, however; a week before Christmas, the House of Representatives voted on four articles of impeachment against Clinton. Two passed—one alleging that the President committed perjury, one that he obstructed justice. To no one's surprise, the vote fell mostly along party lines. The matter would move to the Senate during the first weeks of 1999.

Net Profit

The only real respite from the continuing Clinton scandal came during the baseball season, as Mark McGwire and Sammy Sosa chased Roger Maris' seasonal home run record. Their record-setting seasons (McGwire finished with seventy; Sosa with sixty-six) inspired a renewed interest in the game, even though McGwire came under criticism for using androstenedione, a dietary steroid supplement.

In other sports news, the Chicago Bulls won their third straight NBA championship in the spring, but a players' strike pre-empted the entire basketball schedule for the fall. Dennis Rodman kept himself by marrying TV babe Carmen Electra in a civil ceremony in Las Vegas. Rodman's publicist immediately sent out a press release stating that Electra had coerced a drunken Rodman into marriage, a charge Rodman denied.

Rat Pack Rendezvous Closes

On the subject of Vegas weddings, the Aladdin Hotel—site of Elvis and Priscilla's 1968 wedding—was demolished in April to make way for a new resort, due to open in the year 2000. While the Aladdin was never one of the jewels of the Vegas "strip," it was one of the few casinos remaining from the Rat Pack era. Ironically, just as Americans were becoming more interested in that period of Vegas history, the city razed all but the last

TOP ALBUMS

Titanic
soundtrack

CELINE DION
Let's Talk About Love

BACKSTREET BOYS
Backstreet Boys

City of Angels
soundtrack

SHANIA TWAIN
Come On Over

remnants of its golden era. But with the gambling mecca almost exclusively given over to theme hotels (Hard Rock, Excalibur, Treasure Island, New York New York), it seemed like it would be be just a matter of time before somebody opened a Rat Pack-styled joint.

Cartoons Are In As Comics Bow Out

Just months after it debuted on Comedy Central, *South Park*, the crudely animated cartoon that revolved around four foul-mouthed elementary schoolers, made it onto the covers of *Newsweek, Spin,* and *Rolling Stone*. Along with Mike "Beavis and Butthead" Judge's new series, *King of the Hill, South Park* was the most popular cartoon on nighttime TV; by the end of the year, even toupee-wearing newscasters were fishing for laughs by blurting out, "Ohmigod, they killed Kenny!"

Another show which crossed demographic lines was **Dawson's Creek**, a teen soap which dealt frankly with sexual issues and

elevated young Katie Holmes to stardom. **The Jerry Springer Show** was now the most popular syndicated talk show in the country, thanks to a booking policy that seemed to encourage both the sleaziest topics and the most violent confrontations.

Coming under fire for his show's violent content, Springer promised he'd tone it down, but never seemed to get around to doing it.

After eight years on the air, **Jerry Seinfeld** decided to call it quits, much to the chagrin of millions of fans

around the country. The script for the show's final broadcast was subject of much hype, conjecture, and secrecy, with various fake scripts floating around on the Internet; but in the end, the May 14 finale was largely judged to be a letdown. The spring season also marked the end of the road for **Ellen**; low ratings, as well as a continuing battle between the show's producers and ABC over Ellen's "gay content," apparently contributed to the network's decision to pull the plug. Also getting the hook was *The Magic Hour*, a talk show hosted by former basketball great Magic Johnson, which was yanked after only eight weeks on the air.

Hollywood Fare Lukewarm To Hot

Wag the Dog, released in late '97, received a new lease on life thanks to the Monica Lewinsky scandal and the concurrent situation in Iraq. In the film, Dustin Hoffman played a director hired to film a phony war in order to distract the American public from a presidential scandal. Would President Clinton bomb Iraq in order to achieve a similar purpose? Americans could only wait and see.

Lost In Space was the first film of the year to best *Titanic* in the weekly box-office tallies, despite predominantly lukewarm reviews; many wondered if there were any old TV shows left for Hollywood to recycle. Of course, for a full-on nostalgic experience, you couldn't beat the twentieth-anniversary re-release of *Grease*; in packed multiplexes across the country, Americans were doing the hand jive and singing along. *Primary Colors*, starring John Travolta as a

Clintonesque president, had the misfortune to open the same week as *Grease*; even with the Lewinsky scandal adding extra marquee value to *Primary Colors*, moviegoers preferred to pay money to see the younger, buffer Travolta of twenty years earlier.

1998 featured not one but two meteor-hits-the-earth films— *Armageddon* and *Deep Impact*; it also made way for **Godzilla**, the first Godzilla film to not use a man dressed in a latex lizard suit. Sporting a budget of a hundred and twenty million dollars, the film was trashed by critics but did quite well at the box office. Other big hits included Steven Spielberg's World War Two film *Saving Private Ryan*; *City of Angels*, a blatant *Wings of Desire* rip-off; two Adam Sandler vehicles, *The Waterboy* and 1980s nostalgia comedy *The Wedding Singer*; *Lethal Weapon 4*; *Dr Dolittle*, starring Eddie Murphy in the title role; gross-out comedy *There's Something about Mary*; and **The Truman Show**, which starred Jim Carrey as a man whose every waking move was surreptitiously followed by TV cameras.

Teensploitation films continued to rake in the cash, with *I Know What You Did Last Summer*, *The Faculty,* and *Wild Things* (the latter featuring a much remarked-upon three-way sex scene with Matt Dillon, Neve Campbell, and Denise Richards) heading the list. But while Gwyneth Paltrow may have racked up a mantelful of awards for her performance in *Shakespeare in Love*, **Christina Ricci**, who played vastly different characters in *Buffalo 66*, *The Opposite of Sex*, and *Pecker*, was generally considered to be the indie-film babe of the year.

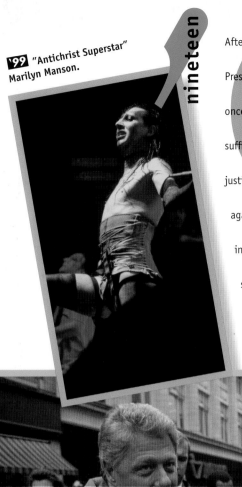

nineteen

'99

After building steam throughout 1998, the impeachment proceedings against President Clinton finally sputtered to a halt six weeks into 1999. With the votes once again falling along partisan lines, Republicans could not muster the sufficient majority to convict the President of committing perjury or obstructing justice. In the eyes of Clinton's detractors, "Slick Willie" had once again wiggled his way out of trouble, an indication that the country's "moral standards" had hit an all-time low; his supporters, on the other hand, were happy the country was finally "moving on."

Opposing Forces

Other conversations in the nation's capitol concerned the possibility of Hillary Clinton running for Senator of New York in 2000, as well as the upcoming presidential elections. Several Republicans, including Bob Dole's wife Liddy, were said to have their hats in the ring, while Vice-President Gore and Senator Bill Bradley looked set to duke it out in the Democratic primaries. More pressing, however, was the worsening situation in **the Balkans**; as March drew to a close, NATO forces began air strikes against Kosovo, but government officials and American voters were still divided over whether or not the US should send ground troops.

Movie News

None of the above debates were quite as heated as those surrounding *Episode 1: The Phantom Menace*, however. Previews of the *Star Wars* prequel had been shown in selected theaters before screenings of the otherwise unremarkable *Meet Joe*

For his part, the President—whose current public approval rating of sixty-six percent was the second highest during his tenure—made a solemn vow to spend the rest of his time in office attending to "the people's business."

The scandal didn't suddenly dry up and blow away, however. **Monica's Story**, Lewinsky's perspective on the scandal, became an immediate best-seller; her giggly appearance on Barbara Walters' March special pulled in so many female viewers that some media watchers dubbed it "the Super Bowl for women."

Flynt Digs Up Dirt

After vowing for many months to "reveal the hypocrisy" of politicians who publicly denounced Clinton's affair with Lewinsky, *Hustler* publisher Larry Flynt put out his "Flynt Report," which featured plenty of dirt on Bob Barr, Henry Hyde, Newt Gingrich, Mary Bono (who was elected to the House of Representatives after her husband, singer/politician Sonny Bono, was killed in a 1998 skiing accident), and several others.

'99 Clinton gets back to the people.

Black and *Wing Commander*, and it seemed as if everyone had an opinion about them. Some said that the star, nine-year-old Jake Lloyd, couldn't act; others opined that the computer-generated special effects looked cheesy. In any case, the film—and accompanying merchandise—seemed set to do record-breaking business.

Teensploitation films kept up their reign of terror at the box office, with *Jawbreaker*, *Cruel Intentions*, *10 Things I Hate About You*, *Never Been Kissed*, *Varsity Blues*, *She's All That*, and *Go* (the only one of the bunch to receive positive reviews) all raking in truckloads of cash. Less successful were **200 Cigarettes**, MTV Films' inept attempt to drum up some nostalgia for the "New Wave" era, and **The Mod Squad**, a TV rehash so dead on arrival that even a Levi's merchandising tie-in couldn't save it.

Some of the year's early winners (at least in terms of ticket sales) included *Forces of Nature*, a romantic comedy with Ben Affleck and Sandra Bullock; *The Matrix*, a cyber-thriller with Keanu Reeves and Laurence Fishburne; *EDtv*, a Ron Howard-directed comedy suspiciously similar to *The Truman Show*; and *Life*, a "bittersweet" comedy with Eddie Murphy and Martin Lawrence. But at last check, all the groovy guys and gals were still saving their money for the forthcoming *Austin Powers: The Spy Who Shagged Me*.

Abnormal TV Success

There was little in the way of remarkable new programming in 1999, save for HBO's *The Sopranos*, which starred James Gandolfini as a New Jersey mob capo on Prozac. An immediate cult hit, the show was far more intelligent and humorous than anything else on TV. Comedian **Norm MacDonald**, recently fired from *Saturday Night Live*, returned with his own sitcom, *The Norm Show*, while former child star Alyssa Milano and former über-bitch Shannen Doherty rebounded as well-meaning witches with expensive wardrobes on *Charmed*. But "Most Surprising Comeback" award had to go to **Pamela Anderson Lee**, whose *VIP*—a campy *Charlie's Angels* knock-off with a bigger explosives budget—completely trounced *Baywatch* in the ratings.

Cartoon Cornucopia

There also seemed to be an abundance of prime-time animated shows on the tube in '99; joining *The Simpsons*, *King of the Hill*, and the rapidly-deteriorating *South Park* were *Family Guy*, *Dilbert*, *The PJs*, and *Futurama*, the new futuristic comedy by *Simpsons* creator Matt Groening. The Cartoon Network's *Powerpuff Girls* were a big daytime hit with the kids, while Britain's *Teletubbies* got on the wrong side of right-wing Christian leader Jerry Falwell, who accused "Tinky-Winky" of being a homosexual. (The purse was apparently the tip-off.)

Making Moral Judgments

In other daytime TV news, *Judge Judy* proved so popular that several other networks rushed out their own courtroom shows; Ed Koch, formerly the mayor of the largest city in the US, could now be seen banging a gavel on a revival of *The People's Court*. And in protest at *Jerry Springer*'s high ratings—and of "trash TV" in general—Oprah Winfrey announced that she would be leaving talk TV when her current contract expired.

Music News

With the exception of records by rap artists like DMX, TLC, Eminem, The Roots, Redman, and C-Murder—and the almost weekly arrests of Wu-Tang Clan member Ol' Dirty Bastard—there wasn't much interesting happening in American music, either. **Bubblegum** was back in a big way, with teen wet-dream Britney Spears outselling the already popular 'N Sync and Backstreet Boys. Hungry for another piece of the action, former New Kids on the Block Jordan Knight and Joey McIntyre released new albums; if they didn't sell as well as their old stuff, at least they could be content in the knowledge that they'd outsold *Hard To Swallow*, Vanilla Ice's aptly-named 1998 comeback attempt. The much-ballyhooed **Marilyn Manson**/Hole tour collapsed after less than two weeks, the victim of poor ticket sales, monetary disputes, and a fall that injured Manson's leg; at least Manson's engagement to actress Rose MacGowan, supposedly already pregnant with his child, seemed like something the "Antichrist Superstar" could be happy about. The "Hard Knock Life Tour," with Jay-Z, Redman, and Method Man, was the first successful hardcore rap tour in years; as spring progressed, however, the organizers of Woodstock '99 still hadn't nailed down any rap acts to join the already-confirmed likes of Jewel, Alanis Morissette, Rage Against the Machine, Korn, Aerosmith, and John Fogerty for the summer event.

Mostly, talk around the music industry concerned the availability of MP3 music files on **the Internet**, with many pundits predicting the end of the industry as we know it. Many online music stores now also included a feature where you could make your own CD mix from a database of one hundred thousand songs. With CD burners priced ever cheaper, and a

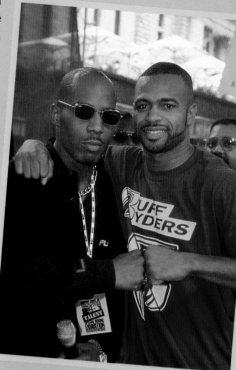

'99 DMX

growing number of cyber-savvy musicians looking to circumvent the hassles of record labels, it seemed that retail record chains could soon be a thing of the past.

US Bugged By Millennium Threat

In other cyber-news, new studies showed that a distressing number of government agencies were still unprepared for the Y2K bug, which was expected to muck up computers not already programmed to make the transition to the new millennium. In addition to debating whether 2000 or 2001 would mark the "real" beginning of the millennium, many Americans pondered the effect the Y2K bug would have upon daily life. Would airplanes fall out of the sky? Would there be food shortages and rioting in the streets? Or would life continue pretty much as we now knew it, with only a few minor complications to mark the changing of the decade? We could only wait and see.

AMERICAN BEAUTY

Index

A

Adidas 17
Aladdin Hotel 41
Albert, Marv 35
Allen, Tim 24
Allen, Woody 18–9
Ally McBeal 35, *35*
Alternative lifestyles 19
Alternative rock 21
Amateur porn 12
America Online 9
American Beauty 46
Anderson Lee, Pamela 15, 45
Anderson, Gillian 19, *19*
Apple, Fiona 32
Arch Deluxe 33
Atari 13

B

Bailey, F Lee 26
Balkans crisis 44
Bandai 38, *39*
Banned In The USA 6
Barbie 38
Barbieri, Paula 26
Barney & Friends 14–15, *14*
Batman Forever 28
Baywatch 15, *15*
Beavis and Butthead 18
Beck 30
Becky 38
Beverly Hills 90210 8, 24
Black Or White 13
Bobbitt, John Wayne 18
Bobbitt, Lorena 18
Bochco, Steven 20, 29
Body-piercing 19
Bodyguard, The 16
Boone, Pat 36
Brown, Murphy 14
Bubblegum 45
Bud Dry 9
Budweiser Ice Draft 18
Buffy the Vampire Slayer 35
Bugs Bunny 32
Bungee jumping 17, *17*
Burns, George 33
Bush, George 14
Buttafuocco, Joey 16, 20

C

Cabbage Patch Snacktime Kids 33
Cameron, James 36
Campbell, Naomi 25, *25*
Carrey, Jim 7, *7*, 24
Carson, Johnny 16
Cartoon cornucopia 45
Chicago Bulls 13, 21, 41
Christian Coalition 14
Cigars 29
Cincinnati Contemporary Art Center 6
Cincinnati Reds 21
Clark, Marcia 26
Clay, Andrew Dice 7
Clerks 24
Clinton, Bill 14, 30, 40–1, *40*, 44, *44*
Clinton, Hilary 44
Clooney, George 23

Clueless 28
Cobain, Kurt 13, 24
Cochran, Johnnie 26
Communications Decency Act 29
Coombs, Sean "Puff Daddy" 36, *36*
Cosby Show 15
Costner, Kevin 10, *10*, *11*
Cowlings, Al 22, 26
Cracked Rear View 26–7
Croft, Lara 33
Crow, Sheryl 27
Crow, The 20
Cruise, Tom 32
Culkin, Macaulay 8
Cyber Porn 28
Cybercafes 29
Cybill 29, *29*

D

Darden, Christopher 26
Davis, Sammy, Jr. 8
Dawson's Creek 42
DeGeneres, Ellen 20, 34, 35, *35*
Desert Storm 10
DiCaprio, Leonardo 36
DMX 45, *45*
Doc Martens 24, *24*
Dodge Viper 17
Dogg, Snoop Doggy 18, 30
Doherty, Shannon 24
Dole, Bob 30, 33, 41
Don't ask, don't tell policy 19
Drugs don't work 18
Duchovny, David 19, *19*

E

Eazy-E 28
Eddie (*Frasier*) 20
Eidos Interactive 33
El Niño 40
Electra, Carmen 41
Electronic music 36
Ellen 20, 34, 35, 43
ER 23, *23*
Etheridge, Melissa 19
Evita 30, 32
Exon, Jim 29

F

Fargo 32
Farley, Chris 38
Fashion Cafe 25
Fay, Michael 23
Fisher, Amy 20
Fleiss, Heidi 18
Flockhart, Calista 35, *35*
Food and Drug Administration 33
Foster, Jodie 12
Frasier 20, *20*
Fried Green Tomatoes 12
Friends 23, *23*
Fuhrman, Mark 26

G

Gangsta Rap 21
Garcia, Jerry 28
Gays 19
Gellar, Sarah Michelle 35
General Motors Saturn 6

Generation X 17
Ghost 9, *9*
Gingrich, Newt 41
Godzilla 43
Gooding, Cuba 32
Gore, Al 30
Grammer, Kelsey 20, *20*
Grease 43
Grier, Pam 36, *38*
Groening, Matt 8
Grunge 13
Gulf War 10

H

Hanks, Tom 21
Harding, Tonya 23
Harrelson, Woody *25*
Heche, Anne 34, 35
Henson, Jim 8
Hercules–The Legendary Journeys 29
Herman, Pee Wee 12
Heroin 7
HIV 13
Hole 24
Home Alone 8
Hoop Dreams 25
Hootie and the Blowfish 26–7
HORDE, The 17
Houston, Whitney 16
Hussein, Sadam 10, 40

I

Impeachment 41
In Living Color 7, *7*
In Utero 21
Independence Day 30, 32
Internet 9, 28–9, 45
Interview with the Vampire: The Vampire Chronicles 25
Iron John 12
Ito, Judge Lawrence 26

J

Jackie Brown 36, *38*
Jackson, Michael 13, 18, 22, 26
Jackson, Samuel L 24
Jenny 35
Jenny Jones Show 29
Jerry Springer Show, The 43
Jewel 32
JFK 10, *10*
Johnson, Michael 13
Jones, Paula 25
Jordan, Michael 13, 21, 32
Judge Judy 45
Jurassic Park 20, *21*

K

Kaelin, Brian "Kato" 26
Kerrigan, Nancy 23
King of the Hill 42
Kiss 32
Klein, Joe 30
Kriss Kross 16

L

LA riots 14
Lambada 9
lang, kd 19
Larry Sanders Show 15–6

Lee, Brandon 20–1
Lee, Sara 25
Lee, Spike 16
Leno, Jay 16
Lesbians 19
Letterman, David 16, 19
Lewinsky, Monica 40–1, *41*, 44
Lewis, Juliette *25*
Lilith Fair 36
Linklater, Richard 10, 12
Lion King, The 24
Lloyd, Jake 45
Lopes, Lisa "Left Eye" 24
Los Angeles Lakers 13
Love, Courtney 24
Lynch, David 8

M

MacDonald, Norm 45
Madonna 30
Maguire, Jerry 32
Malcolm X 16, *16*
Mancini, Henry 24
Manson, Marilyn 36, *44*, 45
Mapplethorpe, Robert 6
Marijuana 18
Mattel 38
MC Hammer 7
McDonald's 33
McGwire, Mark 41
McPherson, Elle 25, *25*
Melrose Place 15
Menendez, Erik and Lyle 18
Mighty Morphin Power Rangers 19, *19*
Milli Vanilli 6, *7*
Miss America Pageant 35
Mod Squad, The 47
Monica's Story 44
Monicagate 41
Moore, Demi 9, *9*, 28, 32–3
Morissette, Alanis 27, *27*, 32
Morvan, Fabrice 7
Mother Love Bone 7
Motley Brue 36
Murder One 29
Murder rates 6
My Own Private Idaho 12

N

Natural Born Killers 24, *25*
NC-17 certification 8
Nevermind 13
Nintendo 9, 12–13
Nirvana 13, 21
No Doubt 30
Northern Exposure 12

O

Olestra 33

P

Paltrow, Gwyneth 43
Parker, Noelle 16
Perot, H Ross 14, 30
Philadelphia 20, 21
Phoenix Suns 21
Phoenix, River 12, 18
Pilatus, Rob 7
PlayStation 29

Population boom 6
Pot-leaf insignias 18
Powell, General Colin 10
Presley, Lisa Marie 22, 26
Primary Colors 30
Prodigy 36
Puff Daddy 36, *36*
Pulp Fiction 24

Q

Quayle, Dan 14

R

Rachel 23
Recession 6, 10, 14
Reeves, Keanu 12
Ren and Stimpy 12, *13*
Reservoir Dogs 16, *16*
Reynolds, Burt 38
Ricci, Christina 43
Rison, Andre 24
Roberts, Julia 9
Robertson, Pat 14
Robin Hood: Prince of Thieves 10, *11*
Rock and Roll Hall of Fame 27
Rodman, Dennis 41
Roswell, NM, 34

S

Saturday Night Live 7
Saturn (GM) 6
Schindler's List 20, *21*
Schmitz, Jonathan 29
Schott, Marge 21
Schwarzenegger, Arnold 9
Schwarzkopf, General Norman 10
Sega 13
Seinfeld 12, *12*
Seinfeld, Jerry 12, 43
Selena 28
Sexual witch-hunt 41
Shakespeare In Love 43, *43*
Shakur, Tupac 28
Shandling, Gary 15
Shapiro, Robert 26
Shepherd, Cybill 29, *29*
Show me the money! 32
Silence of the Lambs, The 12
Silverstone, Alicia 19, 28
Simpson, OJ 22–3, *22*, 26, *26*
Simpsons, The 8, *8*
Ska 30
Slacker 10, 12
Sleepless in Seattle 21
Smith, Anna Nicole 20, *20*
Sonic the Hedgehog 13
Sony 29
Sosa, Sammy 41
South Park 42
Space Age Bachelor Pad Music 24
Space Jam 32
Spielberg, Steven 20, *21*
Springer, Jerry 43
Star Trek: Voyager 29, *29*
Star Wars Episode 1: The Phantom Menace 44
Starbucks 29

Starr, Kenneth, 40, 41
Striptease 32
Supermodels 25, *25*
Surfing the net 29
Swayze, Patrick 9, *9*
Swing 30
Swords-'n'-sorcery 29

T

Tamagotchi 38, *39*
Tarantino, Quentin 16
Techno-thriller 28
Teenage Mutant Ninja Turtles 8, *9*
Teensploitation 45
Telecommunications Act 32
Thelma and Louise 12, *12*
Third Rock from the Sun 32, 33
Tickle Me Elmo 33, *33*
Titanic 36, *36*
Tomb Raider 33
Toy Story 28, *28*
Travolta, John 24
Trial of the Century 26, *26*
Tripp, Linda 41
Truman Show, The 43
Twin Peaks 8
Twister 32
2 Live Crew 6
200 Cigarettes 45

U

UFOs 34, *34*
UN inspections 40

V

Vanilla Ice 7, 10
Ventura, Governor Jesse "The Body" 41
Viagra 41
Viper 17

W

Washington, Denzel 16, *16*
Wayne's World 16
Willis, Bruce 33
Wonderbra 25
Wood, Andrew 7
Woodstock '94 24
Wye River peace accord 41

X

X-Files, The 19, *19*
Xena: Warrior Princess 29, *29*

Y

Y2K bug 45

Z

Zappa, Frank 21
Zima 17
Zippergate 41

Acknowledgements

The publishers would like to thank the following sources for their kind permission to reproduce the pictures in this book:

Corbis/Dewitt Jones, Photo Reporters, Larry White, Ronnie Wright, Everett/*Ghost* UIP/Paramount/Howard W Koch, *Thelma and Louise* UIP/Pathe Entertainment, *Toy Story* Buena Vista/Walt Disney/Pixar, *Independence Day* TCF/Centropolis, *Jackie Brown* Buena Vista/Miramax/A Band Apart, *Godzilla* Columbia Tristar/Centropolis/Fried/Independent,

Ronald Grant Archive/*Evita* Entertainment/Cinergi/Robert Stigwood/Dirty Hands London Features International Ltd./J Bangay, Lawny, J Gordon Levitt, V Malafronte/Celebrity Photo Agency, K Mazur, A Vereecke, *Schindler's List* Universal/Amblin, *Teenage Mutant Ninja Turtles* Virgin/Golden Harvest/Limelight, JFK Warner/Le Studio Canal/Regency Enterprises/Alcor, *Robin Hood: Prince of Thieves* Warner/Morgan Creek, *Malcolm X* Warner/Largo/Forty Acres and a Mule, *Natural Born Killers* Warner/Regency/Alcor/JD/Ixtlan/New Regency

The Robert Opie Collection

Pictorial Press Limited/*Reservoir Dogs* Rank/Live America/Dog Eat Dog

Every effort has been made to acknowledge correctly and contact the source and/or copyright holder of each picture, and Carlton Books Limited apologises for any unintentional errors or omissions which will be corrected in future editions of this book.

About the Author

Dan Epstein is an award-winning freelance writer and editor who has contributed to many magazines. Since graduating in Film Studies from Vassar College in New York, he has worked for *Chicago Subnation*, a bi-monthly magazine devoted to the city's popular culture, and for the *Los Angeles Reader*. He has also had his work published in *Guitar Player*, *LA Weekly*, *Mojo*, and *Time Out Guide* to Los Angeles.